DUTCH ARTIST MADELON VRIESENDORP ILLUSTRATES THE GREAT PYRAMID.

SOLUTION 9

SOLUTION 9
THE GREAT PYRAMID

INGO NIERMANN AND JENS THIEL (EDS.)

SERIES EDITED BY INGO NIERMANN
STERNBERG PRESS

INGO NIERMANN

Introduction

Mankind transforms the planet earth. Of that which can be seen with the naked eye from outer space, little remains but smog and light. Even still, human beings cannot move mountains. They have long had much more mind-boggling things to do. They continue to erect ever-greater buildings, but have ceased to be astonished by them. The monument has become an investment to be paid off in a matter of years. Monumental is at best the alluring façade, while the inside is for gambling, selling, sleeping, or working, under comparatively niggling circumstances.

When Jens Thiel told me in 2005 about the scenario he had discussed with artist Erik Niedling, one that involved building a massive, enormous pyramid in stagnating eastern Germany to ensure—à la New Deal—a symbolic and tangible economic boost, I was skeptical at first. Construction processes have become so automated that the long-term unemployed would hardly stand to benefit. Also, the question as to whether an artificial hill like that could attract enough visitors as to result in hotels and amusement parks before finally becoming a world-class tourist attraction like Las Vegas, Disneyland, or Bilbao seemed iffy to me. Don't the Egyptian pyramids only seem so imposing because they are sitting on a flat plane? How modest would they look in front of a low European mountain range, not to mention the Alps?

Then it occurred to me that the new Great Pyramid, just like its ancient predecessors, could be conceived as a tomb. But rather than a single, exclusive burial chamber, each stone would be a grave. This pyramid is potentially any human being's grave. As monumental as it is affordable, it serves those of all nationalities and religions. Stone for stone, it grows with every burial. Rather than hastily burying one another or allowing our ashes to be scattered, as a small stone in the pyramid we can remain part of our species' constantly shifting and ever-expanding tableau.

Thus the pyramid could become the largest structure in human culture, but would at the same time be a monument of modesty. A monument to one another, since every stone would be the same size and its position determined at random; and to humankind as a whole, because even if every individual alive today were to be buried in this Great Pyramid, it would still be dwarfed by the biggest mountains in the world.

Friends of the Great Pyramid

Together with structural engineer and transport planner Heiko Holzberger, we founded the society Friends of the Great Pyramid and successfully applied for money from the German Federal Cultural Foundation's Future of Labour fund. The 89,000 euros that we were awarded would have to be enough to carry out the first constructional, industrial, and economic analyses, find a possible location, introduce the project in multiple full-length presentations and be accompanied by a film crew for director Frauke Finsterwalder's documentary.

Testing the idea developed an overwhelming dynamic. Jens Thiel convinced us that not only graves but also simple memorial stones should be allowed in the pyramid. Only then could the pyramid truly be for everyone, even long deceased or orthodox Jews and Muslims whose faith prohibits cremation and above-ground burial. Jens Thiel also developed the idea of giving the pyramid a virtual counterpart and refined the project in a business plan along with Stefan Dieffenbacher. Students at the Bauhaus University in Weimar supported Heiko Holzberger by finishing their bachelor's degrees with a technical feasibility study for the Great Pyramid. We asked Rem Koolhaas if he would join the jury for an urban planning competition, and he promptly said yes. He was soon followed by Omar Akbar, Stefano Boeri, and Miuccia Prada, and brilliant architecture firms also declared their willingness to participate. In the meantime, we discovered Streetz, a village in Dessau-Roßlau, as a possible location for the Great Pyramid and were met with both enthusiasm and dismay. The international press gave euphoric reports and many hundreds of people from several dozen countries reserved a stone.

Be it in Germany or elsewhere, the Great Pyramid is possible. So possible, in fact, that in the fall of 2007 we were handed our first charges of plagiarism. Sculptor Michael Bacht claimed that it was one gigantic, perverted copy of his Necropolis-titled model of a modular columbarium. At the same time, our Great Pyramid, as we have recently become aware, has far more important predecessors. In 1997, Bill Drummond and Jimmy Cauty (formerly known as The KLF) announced their plan for an estimated 150-foot-tall Great Northern Pyramid of the People, or People's

Pyramid for short, which was to be constructed out of eighty-seven million donated bricks—one for every Briton born in the twentieth century. And in his 1983 novel *Aladdin's Problem*, Ernst Jünger told of Terrestra, a cemetery that guarantees eternal rest to people from all over the world in the tuff formations of Cappadocia. The promise of powerful touristic effects would prompt a military government to sell the land to German businessmen for a good price, and square urns were developed to ensure a gap-free, jointless layering. *"And so Terrestra could offer a place of rest ad perpetuitatem, the price of which was even lower than that of an ordinary Berliner burial [...] A primal instinct was reawakened. It is said that even elephants go to one place to die, when their time has come."*

Solution

The book at hand is the first in the forthcoming *Solution* series, published by Sternberg Press. I first introduced the idea of the Great Pyramid in fall 2006 in the German *Umbauland*—a slim, seventy-page volume with ten ideas for radical reform in Germany with little financial expense. In *Solution*, authors will also be asked to develop an abundance of compact and original ideas for other countries and regions, contradicting the widely held assumption that, after the end of socialism, human advancement is only possible technologically or requires a yet-to-be-established world order. The great joy that comes from even knowing about the ideas stems from the fact that, in principle, they could be realized immediately. Individual ideas like the Great Pyramid here will be made more concrete in special editions.

The plan to make a series of books developed out of a conversation with Markus Miessen, Hans Ulrich Obrist, and Rem Koolhaas as an answer to a growing flood of readers as voluminous as it is noncommittal. However, when I later told Rem Koolhaas about my title idea, he seemed earnestly alarmed. "Solution" is a word he never uses. He demonstrated how his hand automatically begins to shake as soon as he even wants to write it.

As the saying goes in *Aladdin's Problem*: *"Solutions today are if anything white lies, as they do not fall within the framework of our time: the absolute is not its task."* And yet human beings will eagerly go to all lengths to improve their personal or collective situation—only there is no reason to assume that these solutions, however good, are valid indefinitely. No matter how large or small the tasks they put before them, time does not cancel itself out. The Great Pyramid can, however, outlast all other above-ground monuments, and the human race, anyway.

JENS THIEL

Half-Life

Every year, around one million books are published worldwide. Sixty million people die. Should one of them have done a book, the book will—at least in libraries—survive. If not, most will nevertheless have left at least a grave with a little information on a headstone.

Twenty years later, little more than one thousand of the one million books are likely to be read. Were they radioactive matter, their half-life of two years would make them fairly harmless. Of the sixty million graves, most are abandoned after twenty years or built over and left without a trace. Books, like graves, are transitory. At the moment of their emergence, they appear safe and grand, though in fact nearly all are less enduring than a prefabricated home, lasting not even one generation.

This book is either a beginning or an end. I am convinced that, in either case, it will not be read twenty years from now. If it is a beginning, then the few copies will be very valuable, but its contents will be obvious and general knowledge. The rare reader will be amused by several aberrations that will ultimately have taken very different directions. If it is an end, then social scientists will occasionally list this book as a footnote in little-noticed texts about pragmatic utopias in the early twenty-first century. This book would be altogether unnecessary if we all had not that one question yet to settle: A beginning or an end?

THE GREAT PYRAMID IN SITU. RENDERING BY RENÉ EISFELD.

Responses 2007

"Instant world wonder" –*Die Welt*

"German entrepreneurs are planning to outstrip the ancient Egyptians by building the world's largest pyramid on a derelict site in eastern Germany—which they claim will eventually contain the remains of millions of people in concrete burial blocks."
–Tony Paterson, *The Independent*

"Germans Plan Colossal New Great Pyramid"
–Charlie White, *gizmodo.com*

"Competition for the highest skyscrapers in the world"
–*Bild* Halle/Saale

"A precise copy of the Khufu Pyramid—only four times as large." –*ELLE Decoration* Russia

"The mother of all pyramids will be constructed in Germany to become the biggest necropolis in the world." –Paolo Emilio Petrillo, *La Stampa*

"Instead of being a monument to only a few individuals, Germany's Great Pyramid would be a communal tomb open to anyone regardless of nationality or denomination."
–Candace Lombardi, *CNET news.com*

"Get yours today." –*trendhunter.com*

"Stone upon stone, on its way to eternity in concrete…" –*RTL Nachtjournal*

"People would meet their end with a different attitude. And the funeral becomes a happening."
–*3sat Kulturzeit*

"Rest in Peace—and in Grandeur"
–*ARCHITECT Magazine*

"Germany's Great Pyramid Immortalizes Us All"
–Greg Molyneux, *atlaseditorals.com*

"The pharaohs set the standard but German entrepreneurs hope to challenge Egypt's pre-eminence."
–*The Sydney Morning Herald*

"Pharaonic tomb for all"
–Alessandro Melazzini, *Il Sole 24 Ore*

"Everyone wants to be buried as Pharaoh in the world's largest pyramid."
–Hans Marius Tonstad, *Aftenposten*

"We are Pharaoh" –*Financial Times Deutschland*

"If the team behind it is successful, its members will be rich beyond the wildest dreams of even the most ambitious pharaoh."
–Bojan Pancevski, *The Sunday Telegraph*

VARIOUS

"Millions of people will buy these bricks?"
–BBC World Service

"No, this is not a newspaper hoax."
–Vanity Fair, Germany

"The world grave for all humanity" *–tz*, Munich

"Necropoli of megalomania"
–Thüringer Allgemeine

"The idea could be read as a democratization of
megalomania."
–Andreas Schubert, *Süddeutsche Zeitung*

"Democratization of the final narcissism"
–Florian Rötzer, *telepolis.de*

"I was tempted. After all, all Egyptologists secretly
want to be buried in a pyramid."
–Nigel J. Hetherington, *Daily Star Egypt*

"In the valley of the citizens"
–Werner Habel, *wernerhabel.blogspot.com*

"Wanna be neighbours?"
–ulrikpoulsen.blogspot.com

"Crazy or an ingenious business idea?"
–BZ, Berlin

"Pyramid meets marketing" *–Archinect.com*

"The plan is pretty simple." –*theregister.co.uk*

"So outlandish is the proposal that it has caught the attention of famous architects." –*Deutsche Welle*

"I think it's money-making-scam-ish, but I also think it's pretty damn cool."
–Captain Chewbacca, *stardestroyer.net*

"Ingo Niermann doesn't look like a guy offering tear-the-door-down business ideas for the Internet age. In the first moment he appears almost sheepish, and when asked how it all began he mulls it over as if it had to do with implementing his master's thesis. But the project takes on somewhat bigger dimensions."
–Harry Nutt, *Frankfurter Rundschau*

"Jens Thiel is the motor for the organization: A man with a shaved head and stylish glasses who looks like as if he'd rather smoke cigarettes than waste his time with food."
–Benjamin Prüfer, *Financial Times Deutschland*

"Rem Koolhaas—the architect with the last word, even with this pyramid." –*Il Público*

"Bauhaus Pyramid" –*bldgblog.blogspot.com*

"Mega-Pyramid set to save Germany" –*ORF*

"Typical German gigantomania." –Ropers, *digg.com*

"A pyramid-shaped mass grave so big that it
can be seen from outer space. That's the solution for
a structurally-weak eastern Germany?"
–Johanna Adorján, *Frankfurter Allgemeine Sonntagszeitung*

"The greatest building ever, for all the dead of
this earth. Because we Germans wouldn't settle for
anything less." –Georg Diez, *Die Zeit*

"The Great Wall of China is immensely larger than
this structure, and they buried thousands of bodies
inside for free." –Xquzyphyr, *metafilter.com*

"Of course I doubt this would happen in America
where death is seen as pornographic."
–*anonymousrex.wordpress.com*

"Is the erection of a pyramid of death the only way to
bring an economic boom to Dessau, a shrinking city?
But isn't it a bigger question? Death and dollars seem
better friends than ever these days."
–Momus, *Click Opera*

"Would our German neighbors launch the
construction of Pharaonic projects? Dessau-Roßlau, a
derelict and hardly glamorous village situated in the
ex-GDR, might have found something to guarantee
its notoriety for the coming millennium."
–Thomas Giovanneti, *Libération*

"Death, peace, work, and wealth"
–Liebgard Jennerich, *Friedhofskultur*

"So now the building can begin, as thousands of unemployed people from the west German states are already hot to fill the wide variety of jobs opening in the funeral industry: construction worker, currywurst salesman, florist, tour guide, pastor…"
—*sandramedy.blogger.de*

"Visit Germany and see the Brandenburger Tor, the Hermannsdenkmal and the Dessau pyramid"
—*croydonian.blogspot.com*

"Dessau, a modern pyramid town, not unlike the settlements that grew up around ancient Egyptian pyramids." —*egyptomania.org*

"A whiff of Gizeh on the acres of Anhalt"
—*Volksstimme*

"It's like something from a Black Metal cover: a little German town in the shadow of a gigantic mountain of corpses." —*anonymousrex.wordpress.com*

"A new avatar of Nyarlathotep is slowly emerging in eastern Germany."
—Daniel, *cthulhu.de*

"Until a certain Friday in May, Streetz was just your average small town."—Maxim Kireev, ZDF *heute.de*

"Anyone passing through the little market town of Streetz, a few kilometers outside of Dessau, might overlook a small sign on a fence just past the

city limits: 'Watch out, I might be in a bad mood today!' Had the dog on the picture not been quite so faded, the writing not quite so weather-beaten, one would have been tempted to see this element as another part of the grandiose production that the 'Friends of the Great Pyramid' have been leading since their first visit in May. But then again—and that is also part of the happening's psychological trick—everything is real…"
–Eckart Nickel, *Süddeutsche Zeitung*

"If you look in the direction of the town and try to imagine that a house has an average height of ten meters and the pyramid is supposed to reach 500 meters in the end, then you have a pretty good idea of what that makes us: nothing."
–Ralf Pakendorf, Vice Mayor of Streetz/Natho

"These days in this tiny town of 250 residents, it takes just one little word with a question mark at the end to provoke either a swat with a garden rake or at the very least unleash an endless tirade.
The question: 'pyramid?'"
–Oliver Schlicht, *Volksstimme*

"The project has developed in a very interesting way."
–Friederike Tappe-Hornbostel,
Federal Cultural Foundation of Germany

"A very interesting thing"
–Klemens Koschig, Mayor of Dessau-Roßlau

"It is so nice and economically functional, so clear, so pure, so clean, so logical. It certainly won't be the last."
—Werner Habel, *wernerhabel.blogspot.com*

"We have seven billion people in the world. You can't store them all. Soon we'd have these huge things standing everywhere."
—Klaus Grünheidt, Mayor of Streetz/Natho

"No, believe me, it will never be done."
—Massimiliano Fuksas

"I think it's cool! Will never happen in Germany though. At some point it'll end up in Shanghai or Las Vegas. Unfortunately."
—Hans Zarkow, *rivastation.com*

"It's a trick. They are planning to sell individual gravesites, but it's really just for one person, maybe Bill Gates, so he can be entombed like a Pharaoh."
—Bruce, *metafilter.com*

"If I die in some grotesque way that does not allow for cryogenic freezing, this would be a good backup plan."
—Champthom, *metafilter.com*

"By 30 years from now, it'll probably be cheaper to have your ashes shot into space, anyway."
—Charlie White, *gizmodo.com*

"They use our tax money to pay Jews to build a
pyramid in our country!"
–Metadave, *metadave.wordpress.com*

"It does seem to be another part of the grid.
Germany may have been sitting on important ley lines
the whole time, maybe why so much interest in the
place at all. They may be getting ready to connect the
global grid etheric prison. If this is true, then we are
fucked, even after this life!"
–Thoth, *davidicke.com*

"Well that settles it ... We gotta nuke Germany..."
–Frnnkdlxx, *digg.com*

"The question of where the Great Pyramid should
be built in the end—and where millions of style-
conscious people are supposed to find their drop-dead
chic graves, seems almost irrelevant in light of
the growing hype." –*Qvest Magazin*

"Do not miss the early bird discount!"
–*RTL Nachtjournal*

"The biggest cemetery in the world
will touch the sky."
–Salvo Mazzolini, *Il Giornale*

INGO NIERMANN

The Return of the Pyramid

SPRING 2048. IT WAS IN 2006 THAT INGO NIERMANN, 78, FIRST DESCRIBED THE IDEA OF THE GREAT PYRAMID—A MONUMENTAL TOMB FOR POSSIBLY EVERYONE—IN HIS BOOK, SOLUTION 1-10: UMBAULAND. THAT SAME YEAR, HE BECAME CO-FOUNDER OF THE SOCIETY FRIENDS OF THE GREAT PYRAMID, WHICH UNDERTOOK THE INITIAL ENGINEERING AND ECONOMICAL PLANS, AS WELL AS THE REQUISITE LOBBYING AND SCOUTING FOR A LOCATION. FOR THE PAST 17 YEARS, THE GREAT PYRAMID HAS BEEN THE LARGEST BUILDING (ACCORDING TO VOLUME) IN THE WORLD.

A massive pyramid, when the slope is about forty-five degrees, will never topple over or fall apart—it is the simplest of all stable constructions. Gradually, the powers of wind and gravity can erode the pyramid until it no longer differs from a mountain.

Far more difficult to construct, however, is the stable pyramid with a hollow interior. Here, the pyramid is inferior to a right-angle building. Hence, the pyramid is frowned upon—by adherents to secular functionalism—despite its simple form. The same reputation holds true among those who worship an abstract divinity, as the pyramid's tip rightly points to the sun, the moon, and the stars.

Even if the pyramid is unsuitable to those in search of a functional form, it nonetheless functions as a monument to rationalism, by virtue of its simple geometry. It was, therefore, around 1800—after the high points of Egyptian and Central American civilizations were long since relegated to the history books—that the pyramid experienced a renaissance in Europe. In search of pre-Christian symbolism, pantheistic beliefs also gained ground around this time. The pyramid made its appearance on the face of the United States seal, and a few eccentric princes built pyramids, albeit modest in comparison to those of antiquity. Prince Hermann von Pückler-Muskau erected a pyramid made of sand as his future grave in Branitz, Germany, and King Friedrich Wilhelm II of Prussia used a pyramid to embellish the rooftop of the ice cellar in his "New Garden" in Potsdam.

But the new trend in pyramids lasted only a few decades until the bourgeois revolution came to a halt. With the turn of a new century—in the face of industrialization—and the onslaught of secularization and democratization, the pyramid was viewed as a clumsy form. Society now demanded dynamic monuments that steeply aspired to the heavens— supported by iron in order to look airy.

Only at the end of the twentieth century, as the postmodern widely propagated, did the pyramid form make a comeback. Rapid technical progress and subsequent increased general prosperity enabled the postmodern to resist linear progress. By means of steel and glass, pyramids could now be built that were both hollow and bright inside. Not only the Louvre in Paris but also even otherwise functionalist supermarket-boxes adorned their entrances with half pyramids. Like those of the princes in nineteenth-century

Europe, these pyramids were relatively modest in size in comparison to those of antiquity—a prominent exception being the Luxor pyramid hotel in Las Vegas. And though light fell into the hotel rooms adjoining the glass exterior, the interior shopping mall and casinos remained encased in darkness.

In principle, using the pyramid form for more than just decoration made little financial sense (even by postmodern calculations). With the ever-tapering top, the loss in surface space is by no means compensated by bigger windows. Moreover, the windows of a pyramid slant into the room. Hence, with the beginning of the twenty-first century, plans for loosely piled boxes, which let in lots of light became popular in lieu of the pyramid's more severe form. Take, for example, the expansion of the Tate Modern in London or the Japanese plan for the world's largest building—the highest and most voluminous—at two thousand meters high, accommodating 750,000 inhabitants and some 800,000 workplaces, earthquake- and tsunami-safe, and known as Shimizu Mega City Pyramid.

However light and provisional such constructions might appear, they are as fake—to another extreme—as a monobloc chair trying to imitate a heavy armchair. The form in its audaciously risky towering piles and demanding construction is more irreversible than a formulaic single-family home.

The classic stone pyramid behaves very differently. With the laying of new stones or the removal of the old ones, it can grow or shrink to any size. Decades may pass, in the meantime, without the need for maintenance. In fact, the pyramid is the most flexible and most stable construction ever developed.

In the ancient world, enlargements of old pyramids were undertaken; each, however, was marked with the stamp of eternity. It was not until the advent of late modernism and architectural ideologies such as metabolism that the pyramid came to be appreciated for its flexibility and stability. It stands to reason, then, that the pyramid would follow the function for which it had been known over the millennia: as a gravesite, albeit now no longer reserved for the privileged few. With the growth of the pyramid, yes, it could be a grave for possibly everyone. The ashes of everyone, or from the heirs who so wished, would be encapsulated by cement to create the building blocks, piece by piece, until the day when it would grow to become the world's largest building. And even then, the construction would continue. The stones were so big that they would be difficult to steal, and should construction come to a standstill, the upper stone layers would never erode so much that the inner ashes would be released. Likewise, the stones were small enough that no heavy machines were necessary to help put them in place, allowing the costs to remain minimal. Because of this, encasing entire corpses in cement would not be possible. Furthermore, all new cemeteries would have to comply with taxes and regulations on soil conservation, plus the costs of transferring bodies from distant countries. It was easy to foresee that the trend toward cremation could only continue to grow worldwide.

Indeed, cremation was the final outcome of increasing concerns for hygienic burial in Europe around 1800. The problem became especially virulent in rapidly growing cities, reinforced by an acute deficiency of space in cemeteries. Only Muslims resisted, even though the Koran prescribed no burials, and the main cemetery of Tehran approached the size of a metropolis itself. Yet the devastation of an Islamic mega-city after a heavy earthquake—with no crematoriums available to burn the hundreds of thousands of corpses and to stave off the danger of a plague—was enough to convince even the most pious of Muslim scholars to fall into line. Conceding to cremation, it was only a small step to the stacking of urns, as had already happened in Christianity. Hindus, who no longer wanted to stand in dirty water to scatter the ashes of their loved ones, were reminded that this was a more recent convention.

Persons who were nevertheless opposed to cremation could dedicate a pure stone in memoriam instead. Such a stone could also be acquired even in the name of persons who had been deceased for quite some time. It was only thus that the pyramid could truly become the potential gravesite for everyone. Indeed, these memorial stones would be responsible for the initial growth of the pyramid in its first years, when the idea had not yet caught fire internationally. For many of the dead, several stones were laid by rival siblings.

And so it seemed apparent that no other place and time could have proven better for the construction of the Great Pyramid than East Germany at the beginning of this century. Hardly any other region of the world had less religious zeal, within or outside of the church. Likewise, a clean separation between the Christian church and state had yet to occur in Germany.

In the faint-hearted bourgeois secularization of the nineteenth century, death had been euphemistically equated with a deep sleep, and the cemeteries were pushed to the outskirts—yet for no one is death more final than for the unbelieving. A veritable repression of all thoughts of death, and a way of coming to terms with such irrevocable finality, was to scatter the ashes as widely as possible—from a sailing ship or out of a hot-air balloon.

However, those with little regard for leaving a trace remained in the minority. A compromise regarding traditional burial rules was the placement of anonymous funeral urns in a special cemetery area, or a woodland burial, in which the ashes would be buried among the roots of a tree. That a part of a person's ashes would be found in a tree gave them no comfort of reincarnation, but was at most a symbol thereof. People who scarcely believed in reincarnation at all could ask: Why not give the ashes to a small pig or a pregnant woman? Why not lodge the ashes within something that would exist far longer than a tree?

Some of the bereaved preferred placing the ashes in a sturdy urn or transforming the ashes into a small trinket that they could take home. This, of course, presumed a pertinent family structure in which there would be no question as to whom the relic belonged. Above all, it was difficult to make the keepsake a part of the last will and testament as the burden on the beneficiaries would have been too great. And what would happen if all the people one used to know were also dead? Would the ashes or the worthless trinket just be relegated to the garbage?

The pyramid was the first gravesite that promised the permanent safekeeping of the deceased's remains to everyone: in size and in duration, an endless construction as a monument to finiteness. In the past, people buried bodies in the city, and now a new city has mounted around the graveyard.

With the overall repression of death, the ritual of burials had become a musty relic. In contrast, the pyramid was, quite simply, a classic. The individual decoration of each stone disappears in an ever-growing wall and soon would be covered by a new layer of stones. In a world full of functional spaces disguised as eerie icons, the pyramid makes everything easy. One could take risks, monkey around, whatever.

In the era of Individualism, people still liked to fade into the crowd, like in a wave of stadium spectators, or big-brand boycotts, or web communities without a fixed hierarchy. Through the pyramid, this collectiveness encompassed death as well.

The initial investments were minimal, and to form the stone blocks there was no longer a need for child labor in India, as was the case with the traditional headstones. Building permits were obtained in stages, and the bigger the pyramid grew, the greater the political will grew to make it even bigger. The Chancellors and the Presidents regularly visited it with guests of state, who praised the pyramid as a symbol of international understanding—though ostensibly they maintained their desire to be buried in their own homelands. The pyramid became a regular site for international demonstrations after some political dissidents from other countries were denied the right to a funeral. Various charities provided financial assistance for burial to those without means, and as the European Union operated in foreign affairs less zealously than the United States, it made fewer enemies.

Ultimately, there were only a few golden years in which the Great Pyramid could continue to grow without competition. Partly because the memorial and burial stones that were laid elsewhere—into a wall, dam, or ring, for example—were all, or the most expensive ones, permanently placed outside. Although exposed to the weather, family members could at least approach them directly. And as vitrification continued to improve—enabling humans to be frozen in time—the longevity of the pyramid faced different competition altogether: one didn't die at all, or at least not definitively.

These buildings—holding bodies in transit, waiting for decay to be outrun by medical progress— are not only more fragile, but also potential targets for criminal and terrorist plots. Religious fundamentalists have been up in arms at the blatant attempts to evade the court of God. Family members are trying to attain their inheritance at long last. The courts have been deliberating the charge of murder in cases where damage had been done to persons who had already been proclaimed medically dead. And the churches have been forced to consider whether or not a defrosted person is still a human being.

For their own security, the deep-frozen bodies are kept underground, and the above-ground reception halls—and memorials—are kept in a protection zone. How well they are protected against possible terrorist plots, environmental catastrophes, or power outages remains only a question of money.

In contrast, burial in the Great Pyramid is a commitment to the ideals of being equal and united—at least in death. In one's lifetime, this was impossible—the person for whom it might be possible would not be human. One would rather choose to remain forever dead.

Pyramid Reservations

BEGINNING MARCH 2007, OUR WEBSITE
THEGREATPYRAMID.ORG INVITED VISITORS
TO MAKE A NON-BINDING RESERVATION FOR
A GREAT PYRAMID STONE. OUR OBJECTIVE
WAS TO PROVE THE ACTUAL DEMAND AND
NEED FOR THE PROJECT'S REALIZATION, AS WE
HOPED MANY WOULD REGISTER. THOSE WHO
MADE A RESERVATION APPEARED LISTED ON
THE WEBSITE AFTER THEY HAD REPLIED TO A
CONFIRMATION EMAIL, BUT COULD ALSO OPT
NOT TO HAVE THEIR NAMES DISPLAYED ON
THE SITE. BY MID-MARCH 2008, MORE THAN
ONE THOUSAND PEOPLE FROM NEARLY FIFTY
COUNTRIES HAD RESERVED A STONE. WE
WOULD LIKE TO THANK ALL OF YOU SO MUCH.

Aarin Smith, Vancouver, Canada / Adam Sweet, Belchertown, United States / Adil Benseddik, Fez, Morocco / Agnieszka Wojtyra, Wrzesnia, Poland / Agnieszka Jarmula, Tarnów, Poland / Ahmed Ibrahim, Cairo, Egypt / Akko Goldenbeld, Eindhoven, Netherlands / Albert Hsu, Taipei, Taiwan / Albert Heim, Karlsruhe, Germany / Aleksander Rybski, Tychy, Poland / Ales Motycka, Opava, Czech Republic / Alex Leong, Vancouver, Canada / Alexander Sieg, Berlin, Germany / Alexander Wall, Braunschweig, Germany / Alexander Bertsch, Berlin, Germany / Alexander Schad, Berlin, Germany / Alexander Wolf, Berlin, Germany / Alexander Korte, Berlin, Germany / Alexandra Deichsel, Hamburg, Germany / Alvaro Navarro, Santiago, Chile / Amy Patton, Berlin, Germany / Anastasiya Yermakova, New York, United States / Anders Adebahr,

Frankfurt/Main, Germany / Anders Sjölander, Örebro, Sweden / Andre Vandal, Montreal, Canada / André Fleischhauer, Berlin, Germany / André Stephan, Berlin, Germany / Andreas Pulst, Halle, Germany / Andreas Raab, Weinheim, Germany / Andreas Samuel Admasie, Addis Ababa, Ethiopia / Andreas Schmalz, Saarbrücken, Germany / Andreas Wenth, Neusiedl am See, Austria / Andreas Lohr, Zilina, Slovak Republic / Andreas Loher, Joachimsthal, Germany / Andreas G. Wagner, Mainz, Germany / Andrew Blanco, Bloomfield, United States / Andrew Goforth, Houston, United States / Andrew Morton, Ventnor, United Kingdom / Andrew Smith, Atlanta, United States / Andy Mervin George, Kuala Lumpur, Malaysia / Angela Balgobn, Red Deer, Canada / Anna Nilsson, Orebro, Sweden / Anna Sticksel, Berlin, Germany / Anna Schubbert, Leipzig, Germany / Anne Bretschneider, Berlin, Germany / Annegret Siegert, Frankenberg (Saxonia) Germany / Annette Bouvain, Halle (Saale), Germany / Anthony Hancock, Manchester, United Kingdom / Anthony Shouan-Shawn, South Africa / Anthony Wood, Bristol, United Kingdom / Antje Majewski, Berlin, Germany / Arakawa Akio, Yokohama, Japan / Art Lee, Chicago, United States / Arthur v. Uns, Markdorf, Germany / Austin Mullen, Omaha, United States / Avik Sur, Kolkata, India / Balan Israel Lopez, Mexico-City, Mexico / Barbara Frei, Zurich, Switzerland / Barbara Handler, Hamburg, Germany / Bart Buytaert, Sint-Niklaas, Belgium / Bart Zhao, Wuhan, China / Bartel Scheers, Amsterdam, Netherlands / Bas B., Amsterdam, Netherlands /

Beatrice von Pappritz, Joachimsthal, Germany / Béla
Brandes, Hamburg, Germany / Ben Morales-Correa,
San Juan, Puerto Rico / Bernard Resewski, Berlin,
Germany / Bernd Walther, Döllnitz, Germany /
Bernhard Goch, Mönchengladbach, Germany /
Berndt Zoellner, Dresden, Germany / Bert Buechner,
Innsbruck, Austria / Beth Schmillen, United States /
Betty Kolb, Berlin, Germany / Boggia Mojca, Crathie,
United Kingdom / Brandon Dittmar, Redlands,
United States / Brenda Morrow-Kolesar, Houston,
United States / Brian Mihelic, Redding, United States /
Brigitte Mädler, Biebesheim, Germany / Camila
Vasconcello, São Paulo, Brasil / Carla Kalkbrenner,
Berlin, Germany / Carlos Felicio, Campinas, Brazil /
Charles Hartlieb, Elmshorn, Germany / Chih-Kang
Wang, Taipei, Taiwan / Chris Cameron, Alpharetta,
United States / Chris Vanschoonbeek, Landen,
Belgium / Christel Jahnke, Falkensee, Germany /
Christian Blumberg, Munich, Germany / Christian
Bruckner, Pucking, Austria / Christian Dippl,
Ilmenau, Germany / Christian Girregar, Cologne,
Germany / Christian Hahn, Berlin, Germany /
Christian Jung, Berlin, Germany / Christian Kahl,
Zurich, Switzerland / Christian Kracht, Zurich,
Switzerland / Christian Lanner, Innsbruck, Austria /
Christian Litz, Hamburg, Germany / Christian
Schleicher, Erfurt, Germany / Christian Schragen,
Eisenstadt, Austria / Christian Vaschauner,
Feldkirchen in Kärnten, Austria / Christian von
Werner, Berlin, Germany / Christian Waldner,
Innsbruck, Austria / Christiane Van Wassenhove,
Antwerp, Belgium / Christin Ballenberger, Arnstadt,

Germany / Christina Kindel, Cologne, Germany / Christine Motta, Worms, Germany / Christoph Lajendäcker, Cologne, Germany / Christoph Steinlehner, Berlin, Germany / Christoph Theligmann, Münster, Germany / Christoph Weigl, Munich, Germany / Christopher Berie, Pittsburgh, United States / Christopher Coldbeck, Nottingham, United Kingdom / Ciprian Manea, Helsinki, Finland / Claudia C. Schmidt, Munich, Germany / Constanze Frank, Abiquiu, United States / Cornelia Egger, Neudorf, Austria / Cornelia Mitterberger, Romatschachen, Austria / Cornelius Hummel, Stuttgart, Germany / Cosima Tribukeit, Dresden, Germany / Courtney Blackman, Milton Keynes, United Kingdom / Craig Whiteford, Paisley, United Kingdom / Dan Shaffer, Carmel, United States / Dan Scone, Gold Canyon, United States / Dan Melling, Tryon, United States / Daniel Aurich, Chemnitz, Germany / Daniel Lemut, Racine, United States / Daniel Petronijevic, Belgrade, Serbia / Daniel Russell, Bristol, United Kingdom / Daniel Schenkel, Heidelberg, Germany / Daniel Stummer, Rhyl, United Kingdom / Daniel Windheuser, Erfurt, Germany / Daniel Zawada, Luban, Poland / Daniela Eller, Andernach, Germany / Darrell-Dietrich Conwell, Frankfurt/Main, Germany / David Gomez, Vigo, Spain / David Ho, Cary, United States / David Land, Portland, United States / David Lázaro, Madrid, Spain / David Lieske, Berlin, Germany / David McGowan, Redditch, United Kingdom / David Zieglmaier, Munich, Germany / Denine Hackenberg, Umina Beach, Australia / Denis Marciniak, New

York, United States / Deniz Laun, Bad Kreuznach, Germany / Dennis Erlitz, Berlin, Germany / Dennys Costa, Recife, Brazil / Derek C. Kirchhoff, Minneapolis, United Stated / Derek Duncan, Calgary, Canada / Detlef Samland, Bottrop, Germany / Detlef Franz Nathan Rudolph, Braunschweig, Germany / Diana Kohlenberg-Riechers, Celle, Germany / Dieter Zakel, Vienna, Austria / Dinas Bucas, Vilnius, Lithuania / Dirk Blink, The Hague, Netherlands / Dirk Mieglitz, Halle (Saale), Germany / Dittmar Brandon, Redlands, United States / Dittmers Olaf, Berlin, Germany / Dörte Liensdorf, Streetz, Germany / Dominique Kracht, Neerach, Switzerland / Dominique Matczak, Poland / Doug Miller, Dublin, United States / Eamonn Kearns, Maynooth, Ireland / Eckhart Nickel, Forestville, United States / Edith Chan, Auckland, New Zealand / Edson C. Soriano, Springfield VA, United States / Eduardo Orellana, Santiago, Chile / Edward Jones, Klagenfurt, Austria / Edward Lloyd, Epsom, United Kingdom / Elizabeth Kerr, Pretoria, South Africa / Elsa Wormeck, Berlin, Germany / Emad Ibrahim, Virginia, United States / Eman Nafei, Cairo, Egypt / Emma Russell, Brussels, Belgium / Erik Cabrera, Antofagasta, Chile / Erik de Jong, Nimwegen, Netherlands / Erik Hoffstaetter, Rotterdam, Netherlands / Erik Niedling, Berlin, Germany / Erika Novotna, Opava, Czech Republic / Ervin Miranda, Los Angeles, United States / Eskioglu Onur, Istanbul, Turkey / Eve Hurford, Berlin, Germany / Ewald Eller, Laa an der Thaya, Austria / Fabian Weisbrót, Świecie, Poland / Fabian Dietrich, Berlin, Germany / Fabiano Delussu, Rasun, Italy /

Felipe Zuñiga, Santiago, Chile / Felix Stahl, Cologne, Germany / Ferdinand Tschernitz, Velden am Wörthersee, Austria / Filip Piasecki, Lublin, Poland / Florian Helmberger, Linz, Austria / Florian Brechenmacher, Freilassing, Germany / Forte Ilaria, Berlin, Germany / Francisco Javier Rodriguez Gallego, Huelva, Spain / Francisco Sklenka, Montevideo, Uruguay / Frank Lachmann, Berlin, Germany / Frank Maurice, Berlin, Germany / Frank Voigt, Berlin, Germany / Franz Wögerbauer, Linz, Austria / Franziska Lumm, Jena, Germany / Franziska Necker, Dessau-Roßlau, Germany / Franz-Stefan Geist, Nürnberg, Germany / Friedrich Brus, Essen, Germany / Gary Hall, London, United Kingdom / Gary Wilson, Las Vegas, United States / Genik Jules, London, United Kingdom / George Waring, Apopka, United States / Gerald Gindlhuber, Pucking, Austria / Gerard Vlemmings, Tilburg, Netherlands / Gerardo Marenco, Concord, United States / Erich Gerlach, Copenhagen, Denmark / Gernot Böhm, Gmünd, Austria / Gertjan van Zessen, Kockengen, Netherlands / Geta Cuperman, Pittsburgh, United States / Ghaith Abdullah, New York, United States / Giordano Mettus, Berlin, Germany / Giovanni Bugueño, El Salvador, Chile / Glen Bradley, Morrisville, United States / Glen Lancaster, North Vancouver, Canada / Goh Goh Eh, Singapore / Gregor Robak, Munich, Germany / Grzegorz Witkowski, Tychy, Poland / Guido Bertling, Salzbergen, Germany / Guillaume Schüngel, Keerbergen, Belgium / Gunnar Degheldere, Brugge, Belgium / Günter Wacek, Ferragudo, Portugal /

Günther Deiretsbacher, Braunau am Inn, Austria / Hadelich Valentin, Riparbella, Italy / Haimo Schulz Meinen, Frankfurt/Main, Germany / Hannes Fleischhacker, Neudorf, Austria / Hans-Dieter Lange, Leipzig, Germany / Hans-Georg Urban, Dresden, Germany / Hans-Jürgen Rausch, Wutha-Farnroda, Germany/ Harald Westermayer, Muckendorf an der Donau, Austria / Harald Brörken, Welver, Germany / Harald Bauer, Romatschachen, Austria / Heather Gearhart, Alpharetta, United States / Heiko Holzberger, Erfurt, Germany / Heino Trebbin, Uckerland-Wilsickow, Germany / Heinrich Ross, Burghaun, Germany / Heinrich Boris Fettweiß, Lohmar, Germany / Heinrich Eugen Waller, Bregenz, Austria / Heinz Duffe, Kamen, Germany / Helio Ribeiro, Campinas, Brazil / Helmut Flakmeyer, Berlin, Germany / Hendrik Wolff, Hamburg, Germany / Hendrik Bündge, Heidelberg, Germany / Henrik Svalheim, Prague, Czech Republic / Henry Gwazda, Pittsburgh, United States / Henry Richard Lech, Krakow, Poland / Holger Dölle, Berlin, Germany / Iain Howe, Haarlem, Netherlands / Ian Cully, Dublin, Ireland / Ignacio Molina, Arauco, Chile / Ilja Elias Berthold, Berlin, Germany / Ingrid Eeftinck Schattenkerk, Nijverdal, Netherlands / Ingo Niermann, Berlin, Germany / Izabela Marciniak, Gießen, Germany / Jack Alphos, Cologne, Germany / James Proud, London, United Kingdom / James Walker, Freiburg im Breisgau, Germany / Jan Cizek, Hagenberg, Austria / Jan Claas van Treeck, Geldern, Germany / Jan William Clark, South Amboy NJ, United States / Jana Engel, Leipzig, Germany / Jana

Mehrkens, Berlin, Germany / Janard Lansangan, Palm Desert, United States / Jane Hansen, New York, United States / Jani Kreander, Finland / Janna Lemstrer, Rijssen, Netherlands / Jan-Pieter Mous, Brussels, Belgium / Jaqueline de Andrade Barros, Recife, Brazil / Jared Nicholson, Sydney, Canada / Jarmo Markus Rasanen, Haukipudas, Finland / Jarrod Mann, Melbourne, Australia / Jasmin Lilian Giorno, Berlin, Germany / Jason Schade, Chicago, United States / Jasper Enklaar, Utrecht, Netherlands / Jeffrey Lusk, Lincoln, United States / Jens Becker, Bargteheide, Germany / Jens Koppermann, Hannover, Germany / Jens Thiel, Erfurt, Germany / Jens Thieme, Freiburg im Breisgau, Germany / Jeremy Axvig, Seattle, United States / Jeroen Deflem, Oostende, Belgium / Jesse Phillips, Seattle, United States / Joachim Gebert, Castrop-Rauxel, Germany / Joanne Russell, Glasgow, United Kingdom / João Bóia, Lisbon, Portugal / Jochem Harmen Homminga, Amsterdam, Netherlands / Johanna Koch, Heidelberg, Germany / John Hopkins, Sarasota, United States / John Voakes, Seattle, United States / John-Dylan Bierman, British Columbia, Canada / Jonas Obleser, London, United Kingdom / Jonathan Roscoe, Aberystyth, United Kingdom / Jörg Schulze, Gera, Germany / Jörg Willerscheidt, Paderborn, Germany / Jorge Cortés, Santiago, Chile / Jörn Bode, Buchholz i. d. N., Germany / Jörn Sebastian Basel, Heidelberg, Germany / Jose Gabriel Adarve Camacho, London, United Kingdom / Josef Fuchs, St. Pölten, Austria / Joseph T. Deneesh, Kannur, India / Josephine Colson, Brussels, Belgium / Joshua Davis,

Akron, United States / Jörg Bauhaus, Berlin, Germany / Judith Banham, San Francisco, United States / Juli Holz, Weimar, Germany / Julia Dieffenbacher, Stuttgart, Germany / Jürgen Ostarhild, Berlin, Germany / Jussi Steenari, Lappeenranta, Finland / Jutta Wallasch, Braunschweig, Germany / Kael Schneider, Minneapolis, United States / Karin Stuhlmacher, Hannover, Germany / Karl Köhler, Berlin, Germany / Karsten Becker, Allensbach, Germany / Karsten Erler, Schneeberg, Germany / Kaspar Althaus, Berlin, Deutschland / Katarzyna Kowal, Warsaw, Poland / Katharina Livey, Vienna, Austria / Katharina Bickel, Dornbirn, Austria / Katharina Koppenwallner, Cologne, Germany / Kathrin Kazmaier, Frankfurt/ Main, Germany / Kathrin Neubert, Schönebeck, Germany / Katrin Bucher Trantow, Graz, Austria / Katrin Seemann, Hannover, Germany / Katrin Holzberger, Erfurt, Germany / Kay Stolzenbach, Wilhelmshaven, Germany / Kazunobu Uehara, Tokyo, Japan / Keith Normington, Southampton, United Kingdom / Kenton Kerr, Pretoria, South Africa / Kerim Seiler, Zurich, Switzerland / Kerstin Bollmann, Bottrop, Germany / Kerstin Neubert, Greifswald, Germany / Kimberly Ricotta, New Jersey, United States / Klaus Ehlers, Hamburg, Germany / Klaus Koch, Zernsdorf, Germany /Klaus-Peter Scheffler, Berlin, Germany / Klemens Neubauer, Vienna, Austria / Konarski Christian, Rostock, Germany / Kristian Svalheim, Kristiansand, Norway / Kyle LeBarre, Canton, United States / L. Andreas Zanier, Kufstein, Austria / Lars Schröder, Bonn,

Germany / Lars Wegmann, Lemnitz bei Triptis,
Germany / Laurenz Loki Egger, Neudorf, Austria /
Lee Anne Pedersen, Edmonton, Canada / Leo
Lyonson, Santiago, Chile / Leticia Bevilaqua, Brazil /
Lo Denvy, Singapore / Loa Heß, Berlin, Germany /
Luca Trombetta, Bologna, Italy / Ludwig Schichl,
Linz, Austria / Luís Abreu, Lisbon, Portugal / Luiza
Marklowska, Warsaw, Poland / Lukas Nikol, Munich,
Germany / Lutz Anthes, Berlin, Germany / Lutz
Essers, Berlin, Germany / Lutz Weber, Magdeburg,
Germany / M. F. Fischer, Hamburg, Germany / M.
G. Sajesh, Alappuzha, India / Maciej Budych,
Szczecin, Poland / Magdalena Caruk, Biala Podlaska,
Poland / Manfred Koller, Deutsch Wagram, Austria /
Manuel Gonzalez, Loncoche, Chile / Manuel
Manrique Mora, Lima, Peru / Manuela Jacard,
Santiago, Chile / Marc Frohn, Cologne, Germany /
Marc Van den Noord, Amsterdam, Netherlands /
Marcel Cuperman, Pittsburgh, United States / Marcel
Jahnke, Berlin, Germany / Marcelo G. G. Lopes,
Adamantina, Brazil / Marcelo Silva, Antofagasta,
Chile / Marcin Laszik, Przyszowice, Poland / Marco
Goldenbeld, St. Jacobiparochie, Netherlands / Marco
Ziska, Münnerstadt, Germany / Marcus Wilson,
Philadelphia, United States / Marcy Allen, Monroe,
United States / Marek Rzadkowski, Poznan, Poland /
Margereta Holzhammer, Innsbruck, Austria /
Mariana Bucat, Zagreb, Croatia / Mario Steinkellner,
Germanysberg, Austria / Marion Schorm, Calbe,
Germany / Marisa Colabuono, Pittsburgh, United
States / Mariya Andreeva, Heidelberg, Germany /
Mark Hessburg, Berlin, Germany / Markus

Heidegger, Vienna, Austria / Markus Lang, Bamberg, Germany / Markus Miessen, London, United Kingdom / Marshall Miles, United States / Martin Boll, Sindelfingen, Germany / Martin Ecker, Berlin, Germany / Martin Falkensammer, Wels, Austria / Martin Genzler, Berlin, Germany / Martin Hjort Eriksen, Copenhagen, Denmark / Martin Jess, Halle, Germany / Martin Shaun, Vancouver, Canada / Martin Saarinen, Zurich, Switzerland / Martin Hoffmann, Erfurt, Germany / Matthew Lindner, Dallas, United States / Dr. Matthias Bollmann, Vienna, Austria / Matthias Bruestle, Feldkirch, Austria / Matthias Korntheuer, Dresden, Germany / Matthias Berndt, Magdeburg, Germany / Matthias Karl Wagner, Berlin, Germany / Maurice Fiedler, Erfurt, Germany / Maurice Lagesse, Pamplemousses, Mauritius / Mauricio Sanchez, Tijuana, Mexico / Max Salamon, Regensburg, Germany / Maximilian Stummer, Manchester, United Kingdom / Melanie Feuerbacher, Hamburg, Germany / Melin Leslie, Portland, United States / Menka Parekh, London, United Kingdom / Michael Baumgartner, Graz, Austria / Michael Heinzle, Feldkirch, Austria / Michael A. Defranceschi, Gaißau, Austria / Michael Bell, Bakersfield, United States / Michael Brückner, Berlin, Germany / Michael Brynntrup, Berlin, Germany / Michael Dietz, Vienna, Austria / Michael Griffin, Hamburg, Germany / Michael Jeffrey Adams, Burlington, Canada / Michael Minarzik, Freiburg, Germany / Michael Nyberg, Vaasa, Finland / Michael Pletzer, Vienna, Austria / Michael Ruiz, Los Angeles, United States / Michal Krzemilski, Chorzów, Poland /

Michel Jacot, Berlin, Germany / Michiel Dankmeijer, Haarlem, Netherlands / Mikael Ulverås, Uddevalla, Sweden / Min-young Jeon, Essen, Germany / Miriam Vollmer, Berlin, Germany / Mónica Carriço, Lisbon, Portugal / Muhammad Nayef Pasha, Lahore, Pakistan / Nadja Vancauwenberghe, Berlin, Germany / Nadja Schmidt, Erfurt, Germany / Nanette Niebuhr, Hannover, Germany / Nelson Bland, Chicago, United States / Nici Wegener, Erfurt, Germany / Nick Kutsenko, Kiev, Ukraine / Nicolás Pereyra, Asunción, Paraguay / Niko Sawitzki, Gelsenkirchen, Germany / Nils Krämer, Zurich, Switzerland / Nils Mollenhauer, Leipzig, Germany / Nina Krampitz, Berlin, Germany / Normann V. R. Ellers, Erfurt, Germany / Obriejetan Manuel, Vienna, Austria / Olga Berar, Bucharest, Romania / Oliver Dunker, Leipzig, Germany / Olivier Bronselaer, Antwerp, Belgium / Or Albag, Jerusalem, Israel / Pablo Vera, Guadalajara, Mexico / Pancho Salazar, Lincoln Park, United States / Patrick Martin, Tokyo, Japan / Paul Fruehauf, Linz, Austria / Paul Kamsteeg, Rotterdam, Netherlands / Paul Liem, Krimpen aan den Ijssel, Netherlands / Paul Sheard, Leeds, United Kingdom / Paul Underwood, Mohereen, Ireland / Paul Watzek, Dessau, Germany / Paul Wirth, Vienna, Austria / Pauline Hofer, Torri del Benaco, Italy / Paulo Hermoza, Santiago, Chile / Pawel Dudzik, Tarnów, Poland / Peter Jensen, Vancouver, Canada / Peter Seeberg, Munich, Germany / Peter Simpson, London, United Kingdom / Philip Mörwald, Vienna, Austria / Philipp Sturm, Frankfurt/Main, Germany / Philipp Schmenger, Pirmasens, Germany / Pióro Bartosz, Warsaw, Poland /

Prasanth Bahuleyan, Alappuzha, India / Przemyslaw Koziel, Piekary Slaskie, Poland / R. T. Hansen, Berlin, Germany / Rafael Jimenez Heckmann, Offenbach, Germany / Rainer Schultheiss, Erfurt, Germany / Ralf Straßburger, Berlin, Germany / René Eisfeld, Erfurt, Germany / Richard Söllradl, Pöggstall, Austria / Rita Vanhoutte, Blankenberge, Belgium / Rizos Vassilis, Athens, Greece / Robert Shelley, Houma, United States / Robin Fensom, Wellingborough, United Kingdom / Rolf Lutter, Weilheim, Germany / Rolf Becker, Lüdenscheid, Germany / Roman Lach, Berlin, Germany / Roman Davydov, Dnepropetrovsk, Ukraine / Ronald A. Scheyer, Seattle, United States / Ronald Morales Monsalve, Temuco, Chile / Rucien Le Raq, Bucharest, Romania / Rudi Pircher, Innsbruck, Austria / Rudolf Klauss, Ingolstadt, Germany / Rupesh Patel, New Jersey, United States / Russ Ruttan, Vancouver, Canada / S. Harikrishnan, Alappuzha, India / Sabine Reiser, Nürnberg, Germany / Sabine Kraska, Neuwied, Germany / Sabino Aguad, Santiago, Chile / Sandra Schmalz, Paris, France / Sandra Herrmann, Geseke, Germany / Santiago Balladares, Quito, Ecuador / Schorsch Desmondo, Berlin, Germany / Scott Miller, Palm Springs, United States / Sebastian Uhlig, Leipzig, Germany / Sebastian Jünemann, Berlin, Germany / Sebastian Kochan, Dresden, Germany / Sebastian Streithoff, Wuppertal, Germany / Selina Wögerbauer, Linz, Austria / Shady El Tokhy, Helsinki, Finland / Shaun Burnett, Leeds, United Kingdom / Shaun DeWees, Cincinnati, United States / Shawn Thorson, Minneapolis, United States / Siegfried Protze,

Wolfach, Germany / Siegfried Schliebs, Ransbach-Baumbach, Germany / Simon Deichsel, Bremen, Germany / Simon Sheldon, Cologne, Germany / Simone Birkner, Munich, Germany / Sophia Wögerbauer, Linz, Austria / Stefan Dieffenbacher, Düsseldorf, Germany / Stefan Schroeder, Berlin, Germany / Stefanie Roenneke, Bochum, Germany / Stephan Jack, Darmstadt, Germany / Stephan Pockrandt, Dresden, Germany / Stephan Braese, Berlin, Germany / Stephan Vorholz, Berlin, Germany / Stephanie Franzius, Berlin, Germany / Stephanie Mihelic, Redding, United States / Stephanie Scheers-Hannema, Amsterdam, Netherlands / Steven Moyer, Minneapolis, United States / Stijn Vanderfaeillie, Veurne, Belgium / Storey Ian Christopher, Jarrow, United Kingdom / Stuart Bayens, Edmonton, Canada / Stuart Vaughan Quinton, Pretoria, South Africa / Sudhir Kulkarni, Pune, India / Sunny Rahbar, Dubai, United Arab Emirates / Svantje Heß, Berlin, Germany / Sven Holzberger, Breitungen, Germany / Sven Wegmann, Germany / Tenzing Barshee, Basel, Switzerland / Teresa Ketnath, Munich, Germany / Terje Wilhelmsen, Kristiansand, Norway / Terry Balgobin, Red Deer, Canada / Teumnastra Kühl, Campinas, Brazil / Theo Stiphout, Amsterdam, Netherlands / Thierri Vanbrabant, Willebroek, Belgium / Thilo Folkerts, Berlin, Germany / Thomas Jorkisch, Berlin, Germany / Thomas Josefczak, Munich, Germany / Thomas Kircher, Weimar, Germany / Thomas Landkammer, Vienna, Austria / Thomas Lumm, Jena, Germany / Thomas Pohl, Kassel, Germany / Thomas Schallar, Vienna, Austria /

Thomas Schlick, Bochum, Gemany / Thomas
Schulze, Haltern am See, Germany / Thomas Tunk,
Hofgeismar, Germany / Thomas von der Heide,
Cologne, Germany / Till Huber, Hamburg, Germany
/ Timo Feldhaus, Berlin, Germany / Timotheus
Meier, Vienna, Austria / Tina Margarete Rosenstock,
Erfurt, Germany / Tino Heß, Bonn, Germany /
Tobias Hellström Wärja, Mölndal, Sweden / Tobias
Renner, Dortmund, Germany / Tobias Thomas, Paris,
France / Tom B. Förster, Erfurt, Germany /Tom
Ising, Munich, Germany / Tom Pfeil, Munich,
Germany / Tomas Leyers, Brussels, Belgium / Tommi
Raulahti, Vantaa, Finland / Toni Bauer, Vienna,
Austria / Torsten Blume, Frankfurt/Main, Germany /
Torsten Gerhardt, Kiel, Germany / Tristan Pfeil,
Bochum, Germany / Tyler Kerr, Pretoria, South
Africa / Tyler Richards, Edmonton, Canada / Ulrich
Haage, Erfurt, Germany / Ulrich Hückel, Karlsruhe,
Germany / Ulrich Lange, Dessau, Germany / Ulrik
Deichsel, Munich, Germany / Ulrik Poulsen, London,
United Kingdom / Ulrike Lierow, Berlin, Germany /
Uwe Hetzber, Berlin, Germany / Uwe R. Wieder,
Meckenheim, Germany / Valeria Cancar, Santiago,
Chile / Veronica F., Hong Kong, China / Victor Eng
Linn Ng, Melbourne, Australia / Victor Saldaña,
Santiago, Chile / Victor Schilling, Offenburg,
Germany / Viktor Kutzner, Kaiserslautern, Germany /
Vinay Goel, Toronto, Canada / Vincent Bech,
Balkbrug, Netherlands / Vitkauskas Nerijus,
Širvintos, Lithuania / Volker Zimmermann, Paris,
France / Vytas G, Kaunas, Lithuania / W. Bauhaus,
Ahaus, Germany / Walter Tinkl, Vienna, Austria /

RESERVATIONS

Werner Habel, Mainz, Germany / Werner König, Vienna, Austria / Willem van de Velde, Antwerp, Belgium / Willy-Michael Liensdorf, Streetz, Germany / Wojciech Sikora, Poland / Wojtek Bednarski, Zabno, Poland / Wolfgang Hackenberg, Umina Beach, Australia / Yasmin Wagner, Vienna, Austria / Yiannis Kapodistrias, Kalamata, Greece / Yiovanna Derpsch, Santiago, Chile

Product

Reliable Market

Roughly sixty million people die each year. Demographic statistics provide highly reliable projections of future death cases. In developed countries, about 5,000 US dollars are spent on each burial. We estimate the total revenue of the funeral and cemetery industry worldwide at around 100 billion US dollars per year.

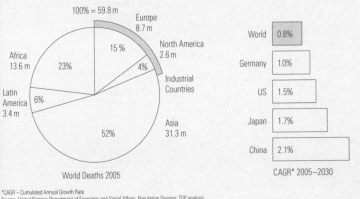

Nearly 60 million people die every year – 12.6 million of whom are in in the industrial countries of Europe, North America, Australia, and Asia

100% = 59.8 m

Europe 8.7 m

North America 2.6 m

Industrial Countries

Asia 31.3 m

Latin America 3.4 m

Africa 13.6 m

15 %
4%
23%
6%
52%

World Deaths 2005

	CAGR* 2005–2030
World	0.8%
Germany	1.0%
US	1.5%
Japan	1.7%
China	2.1%

*CAGR – Cumulated Annual Growth Rate
Source: United Nations Department of Economic and Social Affairs, Population Division; TGP analysis

In many Western countries, the number of deaths is expected to grow steadily over the next decades. Aging people actively looking into burial options will make up an increasing share of the overall population in these societies. Pyramid memorials and tombstones are a meaningful product for many of them.

Not just Western-hemisphere countries, but also China and Japan are currently facing an increase in death figures. Most developing nations, on the other hand, will only see a significant increase in their number of deaths when their current baby boomer generation ages.

Structural Changes Abound

As funeral customs and preferences are changing in many cultures and countries, the highly fragmented industry has found itself under increasing pressure over recent years.

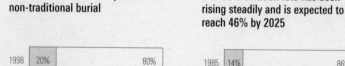

49% of Germans would prefer a non-traditional burial

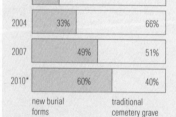

1998	20%	80%
2004	33%	66%
2007	49%	51%
2010*	60%	40%

new burial forms · traditional cemetery grave

The US cremation rate has been rising steadily and is expected to reach 46% by 2025

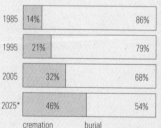

1985	14%	86%
1995	21%	79%
2005	32%	68%
2025*	46%	54%

cremation · burial

*Projection
Source: Aeternitas e.V./ tns infratest, 2007, CANA, Cremation Association of North America, 2005/2007, TGP analysis

Customers have become more price-conscious, initiating globalization in the business. Coffins and tombstones are increasingly sourced from China and India. German families either export their loved ones to the Czech Republic to bury them at half the local rates, or opt for pricey columbaria. In Japan, no-frills burial packages are increasingly sought after.

Cremation rates are soaring consistently on a global scale, with the exception of Muslim countries. As biographies and families become more and more dispersed across the globe, the idea of a hometown family grave becomes less appealing to a growing number of people. At the same time, many municipalities are facing a shortage of cemetery space over the coming years and are looking for more space-efficient burial solutions.

Core National Markets

Taking only individuals with an annual nominal income of more than 5,000 U.S. dollars into consideration, the essential market opportunity for the Great Pyramid is in the realm of nine million cases of death annually.

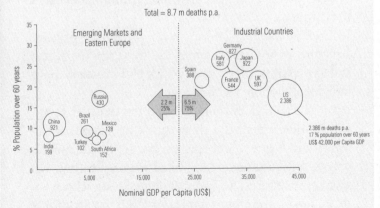

Fourteen national markets provide the largest opportunities

Total = 8.7 m deaths p.a.

Emerging Markets and Eastern Europe

Industrial Countries

% Population over 60 years

Nominal GDP per Capita (US$)

Germany 827
Italy 581
Japan 922
Spain 388
France 544
UK 597
US 2.386
Russia 430
China 921
Brazil 261
Mexico 128
India 199
Turkey 102
South Africa 152

2.2 m 25%
6.5 m 75%

2.386 m deaths p.a.
17 % population over 60 years
US$ 42,000 per Capita GDP

Source: United Nations Department of Economic and Social Affairs, World Bank, TGP analysis

Fourteen national markets provide potentials beyond 100,000 cases.

While the U.S. is, with 2.4 million deaths per year, the largest single national market, the seven largest European markets combined easily exceed that number with 3.5 million cases of death per year. Major opportunities also exist in Japan and China; both countries have around one million annual deaths in the relevant income segment, with very high cremation rates.

India, with around ten million annual deaths, may become a core future market if per capita income continues to rise. At present, only a small fraction of India's population has an income high enough to afford a Great Pyramid stone.

Product Portfolio Overview

For The Great Pyramid to be successful, in addition to diversified revenue it will need to be fused into a broader business system providing additional benefits to customers.

An online platform must represent the physical structure of the Great Pyramid. It allows users to pay real and virtual tributes and also provides information about individuals honored with a stone.

The area evolving around the Great Pyramid will be developed as a theme park dedicated to the legacy and future of our species. It will provide funeral parties with a uniquely dignified experience but will also be of interest to independent guests who wish to explore fascinating aspects of our civilization's tradition and prospects.

The Great Pyramid will be integrated in a comprehensive portfolio of scaleable products securing global access and distribution

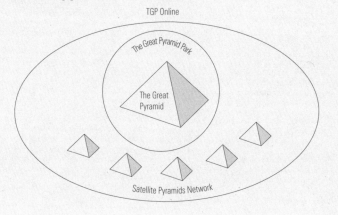

Finally, a global network of Satellite Pyramids will ensure that customers can find their final resting place closer to their native town, but still be part of the Great Pyramid.

The Great Pyramid

Conventional cemeteries are mere transit stations to insignificance, as in most substantial markets graves are rented for only about twenty years and abandoned afterward. Even when renewal of burial plots is possible, families face another steep charge to keep from losing a place to remember their loved ones.

What is more, laborious setup and maintenance, high land consumption, non-standardized processes, and excessive regulations make conventional cemeteries inherently expensive. Cemetery prices have

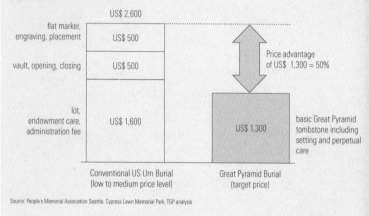

Cemetery costs of a Great Pyramid burial would amount to only 50% of those for a typical urn burial in the US

Source: People's Memorial Association Seattle, Cypress Lawn Memorial Park, TGP analysis

thus been soaring above inflation rates in most markets over the last decades. Stones in the Great Pyramid, on the other hand, are target-priced below most competing burial forms and will endure for centuries to come rather than for just a few decades.

Pyramid Stones

The Great Pyramid opens up new opportunities for honoring a person, and can target a far larger market than conventional cemeteries.

Actual burial in the Great Pyramid is not required to become part of this physical "pixelwall" of humanity, since a memorial stone can be set independently of the actual place or time of burial. The number of these memorial stones may exceed those for tombstones set in the Great Pyramid, at least in the first few years of operation.

Furthermore, now not only close family members but also, for the first time, friends, colleagues, or fans can honor people with a significant tribute that goes beyond placing flowers or wreaths on an existing grave.

Unlike conventional graves, Great Pyramid stones are able to serve a multitude of customers, no matter when or where a person has died or will pass away

		Time of Death	
	Past	Current	Future
Tombstone	Urns from graves being abandoned after twenty years may be transferred to rest eternally in the Great Pyramid.	Status Quo Traditional cemeteries are able to offer their services only related to current and local cases of death.	Securing a stone in the Great Pyramid long before death relieves the family from organizational work.
Memorial Stone	Memorial stones can be set for passed-away family members and also for those we wish to say to "Thanks for having been around and inspiring us!"	Those who prefer to be buried in a traditional cemetery may easily opt for a memorial stone in the Great Pyramid.	A conventional single grave near one's home place does not exclude anyone from becoming part of the Great Pyramid.

(left axis label: Memorial Form)

The success of the Great Pyramid will ultimately also depend on individuals making reasonable decisions about their memorial and burial long before they die. Bookings of future stones as piloted in the evaluation stage will play a significant role in making the Great Pyramid a reality.

The Great Pyramid Park

The Great Pyramid Park will not only serve funeral parties and mourners, but also independent guests visiting the site as a major tourist attraction. Functionalities and spatial planning concepts will have to ensure that both visitor segments' expectations are fulfilled. The park will present history as a series of personal

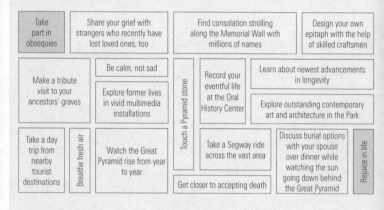

The Great Pyramid Park is as much about life as it is about death

Take part in obsequies	Share your grief with strangers who recently have lost loved ones, too	Find consolation strolling along the Memorial Wall with millions of names	Design your own epitaph with the help of skilled craftsmen

Make a tribute visit to your ancestors' graves

Be calm, not sad

Explore former lives in vivid multimedia installations

Touch a Pyramid stone

Record your eventful life at the Oral History Center

Learn about newest advancements in longevity

Explore outstanding contemporary art and architecture in the Park

Take a day trip from nearby tourist destinations

Breathe fresh air

Watch the Great Pyramid rise from year to year

Take a Segway ride across the vast area

Get closer to accepting death

Discuss burial options with your spouse over dinner while watching the sun going down behind the Great Pyramid

Rejoice in life

rather than anonymously aggregated events. Exciting architectural concepts and a unique atmosphere will attract further guests.

The Great Pyramid Online

The funeral and cemetery industries have not yet found ways to serve customers on the Internet, though experts have been expecting this to happen for years. The plethora of online memorial sites has succeeded neither in recreating the calm atmosphere of cemeteries nor in creating convincing user benefits even vaguely resembling those of real-world cemeteries. Only very few online cemeteries have realized their natural potential for conserving information about the deceased beyond the minuscule bits of data available on tombstones.

Since both advertising on memorial pages and
charging for a webpage with only the most rudimental

TGP Online will provide powerful free memorial functionalities while the site stands to profit from the sales of afterlife-related products and services

	Products	Services	Communication
User Benefit View	**Stone & Tribute Purchases** Customers will be able to easily buy and customize all products offered by the Great Pyramid and by Satellite Pyramids.	**Precautionary Plans** TGP Online will allow users to take precautions for their eventually unexpected demise, e.g. give burial directions, implement postmortem information free of charge, etc.	**Community** Customers will be able to use participative Web 2.0 functionalities, that will help them to collectively deal with the loss of loved ones but also to show their respect for people to whom they feel indebted.
Business System View	**Distribution** Although indirect sales through partners will be significant, efficient direct sales through the online platform will increasingly account for the majority of TGP core and satellites revenue.	**Complementary Services** The platform will be able to monetize on the sales of most various afterlife-related premium services, either their own or those provided by third parties.	**Awareness & Branding** TGP Online will build a large customer base through viral online leverages and be a powerful tool for building the TGP brand independent of the physical structures.

functionalities have proven unacceptable to customers,
all online cemeteries lack a viable revenue model.

The Great Pyramid Online will be able to use the physical structure's prominence as leverage in building the first broadly-acknowledged online memorial site. Users will be able to interactively design rich media memorial profiles for free and find practical, hands-on information about everything related to their foreseeable demise and afterlife.

Satellite Pyramids Network

A progressively growing network of Satellite Pyramids will cater to customers who prefer to have their remains buried in the vicinity of their family or who feel emotional barriers to having their ashes shipped to another country. Engineering solutions as well as online memorial and distribution functionalities once established for the Great Pyramid will be

A steadily growing network of Satellite Pyramids would make the Great Pyramid solution more accessible to customers with regional burial preferences

leveraged into the Satellite Pyramids. These technically identical smaller Pyramids will be operated by legally independent companies. Satellite Pyramids will mainly contain tomb-stones and only few memorial stones. In any case, for every stone set in a Satellite Pyramid, a mirror memorial stone will be added to the core Great Pyramid—thus contributing to the growth of the core structure. The establishment of Satellite Pyramids would furthermore ease the cemetery space crunch which an increasing number of municipalities in various regions of the world currently face.

Toward a New Convention
The Great Pyramid is not a niche product. It creates

value for customers and eases the pain they feel regarding currently existing alternatives. Once commenced, the Great Pyramid can, over the period of only a few decades, become, in terms of volume, the largest structure ever created by men.

A marketing strategy must therefore attempt to make a positive impact on the lives of millions of families and people on an increasingly global scale. Nevertheless, the disruptive stance that the project takes will require some time to trickle into the

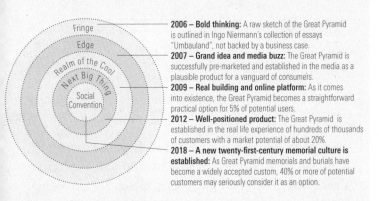

The Great Pyramid on its way from the fringe to the chance for a new convention

Fringe
Edge
Realm of the Cool
Next Big Thing
Social Convention

2006 – Bold thinking: A raw sketch of the Great Pyramid is outlined in Ingo Niermann's collection of essays "Umbauland", not backed by a business case.

2007 – Grand idea and media buzz: The Great Pyramid is successfully pre-marketed and established in the media as a plausible product for a vanguard of consumers.

2009 – Real building and online platform: As it comes into existence, the Great Pyramid becomes a straightforward practical option for 5% of potential users.

2012 – Well-positioned product: The Great Pyramid is established in the real life experience of hundreds of thousands of customers with a market potential of about 20%.

2018 – A new twenty-first-century memorial culture is established: As Great Pyramid memorials and burials have become a widely accepted custom, 40% or more of potential customers may seriously consider it as an option.

Source: TGP analysis based on the DEVOX product cycle model by Ryan Mathews and Wacker Watts ("The Deviant's Advantage – How Fringe Ideas Create Mass Markets", Crown Business, London, 2003)

mainstream in order to realize its full potential.

Facilitating a Movement

The Great Pyramid System cannot be exhaustively understood as a bundle of products, but only as a platform that must focus on the wants of many more stakeholders than shareholders.

In contrast to, for example, open-source software projects, the Great Pyramid as a physical structure necessitates substantial up-front monetary investment. The Great Pyramid can therefore only come into existence when it provides commercial chances as

Be True!

a for-profit business—or not at all. It will be successful, however, only when it is understood that exploiting death and grief is no long-term sustainable business, but that providing fair and good-value opportunities to handle those experiences is. "Be true!" shall provide a simple but powerful business ethics guideline.

HEIKO HOLZBERGER, JENS THIEL

Construction

Inside-Out Growth

The Great Pyramid rises layer by layer. Unlike a house, it has no ultimate size, but grows like a tree in annual rings, inside out from its core, allowing the structure to maintain a nearly perfect pyramidal shape even during construction. In the beginning, stones may be set in

The Great Pyramid rises layer by layer as a self-similar geometrical form

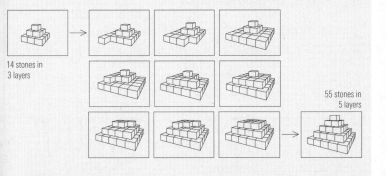

14 stones in 3 layers

55 stones in 5 layers

upward spirals around the Great Pyramid's surface. When the structure has reached larger proportions, more efficient approaches can be implemented: one side of the Great Pyramid may be completely covered with a new layer of stones before proceeding with construction on the next side.

Though older stones will be safely covered by newer ones after a certain period of time, each will be locatable using its own unique coordinates and viewable via the Great Pyramid's online portal. Unlike in a conventional grave, the stone won't be lost and is protected against vandalism.

Foundation

The Gizeh pyramids could do entirely without groundwork, since a plateau of rock provided sufficient stability. Although bedrock would also be ideal for the Great Pyramid, grounding the structure in weaker soil poses no major technical problems.

Technically the Great Pyramid's foundation poses no major engineering problems, whatever the realistic size of the structure

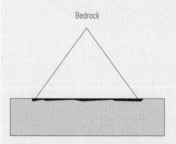

Bedrock

The Great Pyramid is ideally built on near-surface rock where only a top layer of poorer soil would be replaced by a resilient levelling layer.

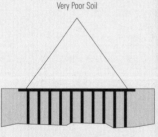

Very Poor Soil

Even on very poor soil, conventional concrete pile foundations carrying a concrete base-plate would provide sufficient strength.

Note: Illustrations, proportions not to scale

We propose a shallow foundation, e.g. a mat slab of gravel two meters thick, to distribute loads evenly across the entire area. Moderate yielding poses no problem so long as it is largely even across the entire expanse of the foundation. Softer ground would need improvement, via vibro-compaction. On very weak soil, a deep foundation consisting of a steel-reinforced concrete baseplate and piles running between ten and eighty meters deep would be a technically viable if costly solution.

Like the pyramid, the groundwork also expands from the inside out. The initial base will suffice for the first years. As the pyramid's boundaries approach the foundation's limits, groundwork will be extended.

Material

Concrete is the only material option for the Great Pyramid. Highly resilient, durable, easy to cast, customizable in most different colors, universally available, and cost efficient, it is the ideal material to safely enclose memorial capsules and urns.

Concrete is used more than any other man-made material. As of 2005, nearly six billion cubic meters of concrete are consumed each year, which amounts to one cubic meter per capita. Even if a Great Pyramid stone is set for every single deceased person, world concrete consumption would rise by only 1 percent.

The specific qualities of concrete are determined by the raw material mix, additives, and casting process. Established concrete specifications meet the technical requirements of the Great Pyramid. The precise composition of the concrete mix used for the pyramid stones will, however, consider technical, aesthetic, and economic criteria, the foremost being long-term mechanical properties, cost, color, and surface quality.

After it has at some point been decided not to continue building the Great Pyramid, the structure

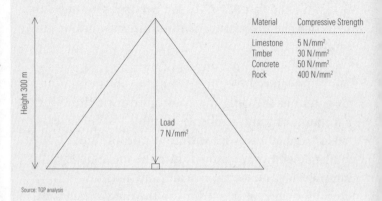

Standard-strength concrete is able to withstand the loads at the Great Pyramid's base without any reinforcement needed

Material	Compressive Strength
Limestone	5 N/mm²
Timber	30 N/mm²
Concrete	50 N/mm²
Rock	400 N/mm²

Height 300 m

Load 7 N/mm²

Source: TGP analysis

could be sealed with a layer of even more durable natural stone.

Stones

Each stone holds a capsule that contains either ashes or small memorabilia in an inner cavity. The stones' contents will be permanently sealed in a compact concrete enclosure. Great Pyramid stones will be pre-fabricated in the Pyramid's economic vicinity. The stones' measurements are designed to suit the pyramid's specific angles and proportions. Linkages will ensure that the stones fit snugly into place when set.

Stones are all the same size, but can be customized with highly-individualized epitaph plates. These epitaphs may be engraved in natural stone, carved wood, or limestone, or even large-format photos laminated between acrylic glass and solar-powered LED-panels.

Standardized stones allow for the necessary process efficiency but can be highly individualized with custom epitaph plates

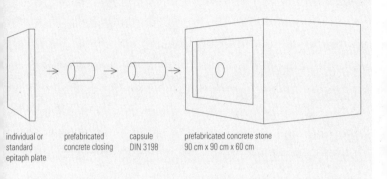

individual or standard epitaph plate

prefabricated concrete closing

capsule DIN 3198

prefabricated concrete stone 90 cm x 90 cm x 60 cm

Funeral or memorial parties may actively take part in a stone assembly celebration that would replace the act of covering a grave with soil in a pre-pyramid sepulcher.

Growth and Capacity

The smaller the Great Pyramid is, the faster it grows with every stone set. A thirty-meter-high pyramid will be raised one more horizontal layer if 2,601 stones are added. Once it has reached a height of one hundred meters, 28,000 stones will be needed to add another stratum of stones.

Capacity is practically unlimited. A 150-meter pyramid can contain up to 5.3 million stones. One hundred million stones will result in a structure only four hundred meters high.

Height, however, is not the decisive factor in terms of the structure's significance. Even with only a

Capacities of the Great Pyramid are practically unlimited

Layers (stones)	Height (m)	Capacity (million stones)
500	300	41.8
400	240	21.4
300	180	9.1
200	120	2.7
100	60	0.3

few tens of thousands stones set, the Great Pyramid will individually memorialize more people for ages to come than any other monument in existence.

Construction

Suitable and efficient construction technologies are readily at hand but will be adapted and enhanced. Since the vast majority (70 percent) of stones will be located in the lower third and only 4 percent of stones in the upper third of the Great Pyramid at any given size, diverse technologies may be employed concurrently. All machinery and processes will be designed or redesigned to render the site a tranquil atmosphere befitting a memorial monument.

Below a height of twenty meters, mobile telescopic cranes will suffice to handle a moderate

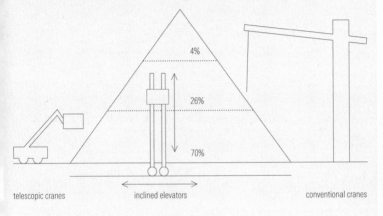

Various efficient construction technologies are readily at hand for building

number of stone settings. As the pyramid grows to accommodate a larger number of stones, conventional or portal cranes and horizontally flexible inclined elevators will be more efficient.

Reflections

The Great Game to Come
Chus Martínez

The Pyramid is like a camp for nomadic death on a planetary scale. If life is an increasingly difficult task, so is death. From the different nationalistic projects that colonize the regions of the developed world, to the desperate calls to join some faith or other in order to baptize existence with a new meaning, to the tragic struggles of thousands of individuals who try to escape extreme living conditions by jumping the "estrecho"—the fourteen kilometers that separate Spain from the north of Africa—it seems that death is a basis for political action.

The pyramid develops from the logic of death's coming to us all and making us all equal in the end, thereby turning this old maxim into a science-fictional commune for the conscious dead. The pyramid, like the family home, acts here as a paradigm for a fixed sense of orientation, a new funerary landmark for the global pilgrim. A pyramid is pure exteriority, a clear universal form that embodies volume and completely isolates its inside world. It is a huge jukebox that can only be played by a revolutionized society. That new skin that thus covers the earth is completely opaque; by definition, the future cannot be pictured. The pyramid cannot reveal what is on its inside. It is not known if it hosts a new utilitarian city for the dead, or if all sorts of chaotic slums are embraced under its appearance of eternal order. There are no windows to the future:

hinting at the pyramid's possible insides may be used as a prescription, transforming the image you could see through those windows into a new official order that again will need to be subverted. The new pyramid intends to give minimum conditions for that future situation of resting eternally together. That should remain as free and open as possible.

The pyramid is an intriguing project. It could be read as a revival of functionalist architecture based on quite reactionary conceptions calling for a holistic urbanism of death, a monument borrowed from an old empire superimposed on the territory of Dessau or wherever it is erected, therefore encouraging a psycho-geographic mapping. But if we take the pyramid as a machine—instead of reading it as a monument—and if we see that inserted form in the city as a device, then the narrative logic shifts. The pyramid, like a Platonic ideal, already exists. It is an ambience of freedom floating somewhere, a sculptural play between mass and void, completely disengaged from the ground but waiting to land in a place in order to finally fulfill a function. The raison d'être of the pyramid is to provide a habitat, a fundamental form, that encompasses life's ultimate form: death. A new habitat that will break with the familiar forms of our communal spaces and their subjective expressionism like the school, the church, the house, the hospital, the station, the shopping center. The pyramid can thus be seen as totally other than the reductive functionalism of the aforementioned constructions. Sure, it is a mega-cemetery calling for the ritual, but the pyramid is also a mega-structural fantasy that emerges as a formal strategy to challenge the trajectory of the present: a random apparition of the future in the horizon machine.

Why The Great Pyramid Troubles Me
Christian Kracht

The Great Pyramid, in seeking to classify and thereby fit the individual into its predetermined social framework, inherently presents the possibility of resisting the subordination that this categorization otherwise facilitates. However, crucial to creating individuality in this environment is our realization or awareness of the possibility of doing so. While this potential for individuality within the pyramid exists, it is up to us to utilize it. Will this work? I sincerely believe it will not.

Through the pervasiveness of mass-marketing and reproducibility, the de-individualizing effects of which Herbert Marcuse speaks have become augmented. Marcuse's potential solution of going underground, of creating individuality apropos autonomous self-definition, is rendered impossible through the construction of the pyramid. The aforementioned aspects of the postmodern condition flattened the vertically-oriented differentiating structure underlying critical modernity into a horizontal, homogenous plane. This horizontality is comparable to an affirmative modernity, though under postmodernity it is taken a step further. That is to say, the potential for creating a unique identity that affords one a distinct sense of belonging or definition within larger society has entirely vanished. Due to the ubiquity of commodification under postmodernity, all manner of identities, including the identity of death (and, indeed, the dying), are, through Niermann and Thiel, up for sale, thereby eroding any differences or distinctions between them. And this is precisely why I am against the physical construction of the Great Pyramid.

Postmodern Utopia
Till Huber

Niermann undercuts the notion of utopia and "de-utopizes" by discussing a concrete realization of each in the here and now. The utopia-constituting element of its nonexistence, implemented in literature through the establishing of chronological or spatial difference from an existing system, is undermined. Aesthetic measures of value are integrated into the call for an offensive reform of reality, though frequently presented from behind a utilitarian smokescreen. Thus *Umbauland* proposes the building of a potentially colossal pyramid as a multi-religious tomb, though what is propagated, in addition to its spectacular architectural and cultural enterprise, is above all its economic function in saving a structurally weak region. *Umbauland* therefore becomes a compromised utopia and, in exactly this concession to reality, dissolves the boundaries of a by-definition fictional genre. An aestheticistic claim attempts a synthesis with a seemingly incommensurate utilitarian logic in order to undercut it in the name of aestheticism. Possibly concealed in this is a desire for the subversive subjugation of an unaesthetic society.

Excerpt from Ausweitung der Kunstzone: Ingo Niermanns und Christian Krachts "Docu-Fiction."

In: Depressive Dandys. Zwischen Literarisierung und Selbststilisierung in der Pop-Moderne, *edited by Alexandra Tacke and Björn Weyand, Cologne/Weimar, 2009 (forthcoming).*

A Pyramid Always Hides Another Pyramid
Hans Ulrich Obrist

In a conversation with Tayeb Salih, the visionary Wimbledon-based writer told me about Gamal al-Ghitani, one of the great writers and public intellectuals in the Middle East today. It was on the occasion of the Egypt interview project that I realized in Cairo on December 24-25 of 2007 that I finally had the chance to meet al-Ghitani. We spoke about many things, and also touched upon the pyramids and al-Ghitani's visionary pyramid texts: the text of pyramids, the pyramid of texts. In al-Ghitani's words: "The ancient historians mention that the pyramids were once covered with a rosy cladding upon which were written words in a strange script. This disappeared but was not erased, its appearance being henceforth dependent upon certain conditions, of which the most important were concentration and the maintenance of observation at specific times. Given, however, the difficulty of identifying these times, it was necessary to look all the time. At a certain moment, lightly, almost imperceptibly, the words would start to appear..." We also touched upon the link between the pyramid and the city, the impossibility of a synthetic image of the city, and the impossibility of a synthetic image of the pyramids. Al-Ghitani describes the structure of the pyramids as too all-embracing to be comprehended in a single glance. Pars pro toto! Certain points can be fixed and others get lost in the totality of the dissolving structure.

Here a list of some of the key pyramid topics to celebrate the accomplishment of the first major step of the Great Pyramid gesamtkunstwerk with more quotes from al-Ghitani's pyramid texts.

ALWAYS PYRAMID
The pyramids were always with him

BEGINNING PYRAMID
Beginnings are an instant,
one containing place and time

CIRCAMBULATE PYRAMID
See visiting pyramid

CENTER PYRAMID
The reason for his presence in the city

CLEAR PYRAMID/OBSCURE PYRAMID
What seems clear on one occasion is obscure on another

DAY PYRAMID/NIGHT PYRAMID
Day is born of night and night emerges from day…
How the pyramid's appeerence changed throughout the
hours of night and day

EYE PYRAMID/MIND PYRAMID
Sometimes the mind will see what the eye cannot, and
sometimes the eye will grasp what the mind cannot

LOVE PYRAMID
Love without knowledge is impossible

MEMORY PYRAMID
Eric Hobsbawm's protest against forgetting

PATH PYRAMID
Each path leads inevitably to another

VISITING PYRAMID
They are for visiting, not for dwelling in

WONDER PYRAMID…

A Cornerstone Cringle
David Woodard

> **"A CORNERSTONE CRINGLE" WAS PREMIERED
> AT THE PYRAMID FESTIVAL BY THE LOS
> ANGELES CHAMBER GROUP, FEATURING LUKÁ
> LINHART (TROMBONE), NILS MARQUARDT
> (TROMBONE), VÍT POLÁK (TRUMPET),
> GRZEGORZ ROGALA (TRUMPET), AND STEFAN
> M. PAHLKE (TUBA).**

In summer of 2007, the Friends of the Great Pyramid
kindly petitioned me to compose and conduct a fanfare
commemorating the symbolic cornerstone-laying of
the Great Pyramid, scheduled for that September at
the proposed Streetz site. The idea of contributing
to this project, which seeks to provide a central
locus for humanity's cremains, compassionately
embracing all religious, genetic, geographic, and
societal backgrounds, seemed a noble cause. I put on
my best face and set to work on a composition that
would be at once stately, pensive, and suspended in
animation, ideally reflecting the joys and humor of life
while acknowledging its tribulations, uncertainties,
triumphs, and ultimate comfort in "sweetest death,"
as Johann Sebastian Bach would have put it. Much

of the piece would, I hoped, mirror life's tragic plays and seriousness, thus resonating authentic human experience and effectively springing the listener's soul from its moorings. Speaking with project ideologues Ingo Niermann and Jens Thiel, I was convinced that the intentions which lay behind the Great Pyramid could indeed manifest in a growing physical structure that serves to ease humanity's collective death anxieties with dignified economy, in observation of our oneness as a species.

Pondering the task at hand, I awoke one morning with the title "A Cornerstone Cringle" ringing gently in my mind—the remnant of an otherwise forgotten nautical dream, perhaps, though at the time I did not consciously know what a cringle was. Christian Kracht had referred to the upcoming event as "a cornerstone-laying ceremony," though according to Ingo the five custom cement blocks to be delivered would be devoid of cremains and together serve only as the pyramid's symbolic foundation, mainly for the consideration of Dessau area residents.

I sat at the piano with exponentially growing questions. "A Cornerstone Cringle," with its long-held chords rendered by five brass instruments, thus launches questioningly from the solitary harkening of the second trombone's B Flat, and develops slowly in harmonic breadth and complexity with successive phrases, sometimes punctuated by a belligerent silence. At its moment of darkness, the music refers back to simpler, earlier phrasings, which sound lighthearted by contrast. Without defaulting to anything more melodic than a circular four-note motif, teasing the listener with the prospect of eternal recurrence, the score proves it was just kidding—delirium yields to resolution in the oneness of the tonic chord, sounded in tutti and held thenceforth, fading, wisened and salved, alone again yet invincible in goodness, to eternity. I picture the treasured final chord as the solitary cringle to which our sails had been securely attached through life, though we were never able to recognize it until the tepid hand of Lady Fortuna had closed our eyes to the myriad follies of worldly illusion.

"A Cornerstone Cringle" was written to commemorate the idealistic columbarium's opening gala. However, a number of attendees at its premiere felt the brass fanfare to be an ideal *prequiem* by which future Great Pyramid internments, albeit those privileged with sufficient foreknowledge of death (for example, persons facing scheduled execution, martyrdom, or euthanasia), might expire with dignity, within the work's four-minute harmonic narrative timeframe.

On the morning after the symbolic cornerstone-laying ceremony, across the now empty central Streetz field, I took a brisk walk. The stage had been disassembled and removed. Seated within the tall blades of phalaris grass, a solitary metal object captured my attention. It appeared profoundly alone in the middle of a field that patiently awaited, with hope and trust, the arrival of humanity's cremains. I walked over and held the object in my hand, fingering its heavy, solid form, deeply moved. It was a cringle.

85

Dedicated with Love and Admiration
to All Future Internments
within the Great Pyramid,

2007

Location

Location Specification

During the evaluation stage of the Great Pyramid project, we limited our search to include only sites in eastern Germany in order to discuss it as a means of creating new employment opportunities in the new German states' fledging economies.

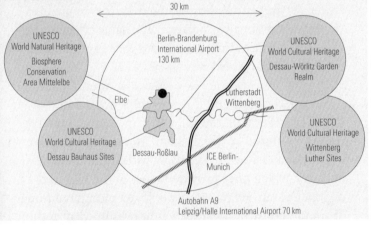

Anhalt-Dessau offers a uniquely dense cultural heritage landscape and excellent traffic connections

In an ad-hoc site selection, we decided to pursue the project in Anhalt-Dessau, a region in Saxony-Anhalt. Encompassing four UNESCO World Heritage Sites, it offers a uniquely dense cultural landscape. Anhalt-Dessau is easily accessible via autobahns, major train lines, and waterways and is situated close to the international airports of Berlin and Leipzig/Halle.

Out of various location options in Anhalt-Dessau, we have chosen Dessau-Roßlau for further evaluation, because the city has a globally acknowledged name as home to the Bauhaus school of architecture and because public officials openly voiced interest in the project at a very early stage.

We have identified the largest open and connected plot of land on the northern edge of the city limits. The area is currently used for agriculture, and is situated outside the Elbe River flood plain. Development of the area is not immediately limited by nature conservation concerns, groundwater protection issues, or industrial sites located in the immediate vicinity. Additionally, "Streetz," the name of the small village adjacent to the site, seemed easy to pronounce for non-German-speakers.

Economic and Demographic Situation

After the German reunification in 1990, Saxony-Anhalt suffered a breakdown of non-competitive industrial activities, particularly within the chemicals industry, which once provided most of the jobs in the region. Dessau had previously enjoyed a long tradition of aircraft construction that was not resumed after the Second World War and was once a major hub for rail car manufacturing. Unemployment rates have hovered at a steady 20 percent for years and the per capita income is still 30 percent below the German average.

To narrow this gap, the European Union Convergence Fund has provided investment grants that have helped Saxony-Anhalt to become a major solar technology cluster over recent years. Nevertheless, the even previously only sparsely populated region has lost 13 percent of its population since 1991. In July 2007,

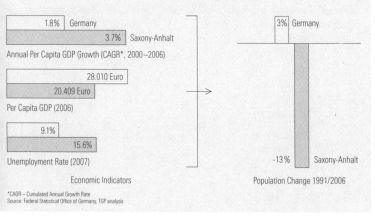

Despite above-average economic growth, persistent structural weaknesses have resulted in a continuing drop in Saxony-Anhalt's population

1.8% Germany
3.7% Saxony-Anhalt
Annual Per Capita GDP Growth (CAGR*, 2000–2006)

28.010 Euro
20.409 Euro
Per Capita GDP (2006)

9.1%
15.6%
Unemployment Rate (2007)

Economic Indicators

3% Germany
-13% Saxony-Anhalt
Population Change 1991/2006

*CAGR – Cumulated Annual Growth Rate
Source: Federal Statistical Office of Germany, TGP analysis

Dessau (pop. 75,000) and Roßlau (pop. 15,000) were therefore forced to merge in order to maintain their status as a county-independent core city.

Tourism in the Region

Despite its unique cultural heritage, Saxony-Anhalt has failed to translate these assets into tourist arrivals. With 31 percent, it has the lowest hotel capacity booking rate of all German states. With only 2.1 annual tourists per inhabitant, it also stands at the end of the line. In absolute numbers, Saxony-Anhalt boasts the fewest international tourist arrivals of all German states.

The Great Pyramid and accompanying park seem to be a forward-looking extension of Saxony-Anhalt's key themes in tourism marketing: "The

Romanesque Route" traces the roots of Western civilization back to the medieval age, and "Garden Dreams" promotes the state's more than one thousand national heritage parks.

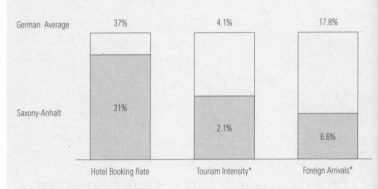

The region has failed to generate substantial tourism so far; crucial indicators are significantly below German average

German Average — 37% — 4.1% — 17.8%

Saxony-Anhalt — 31% — 2.1% — 6.6%

Hotel Booking Rate — Tourism Intensity* — Foreign Arrivals*

*Tourism intensity as arrivals/inhabitant, foreign arrivals as % of total arrivals
Source: Federal Statistical Office of Germany, TGP analysis

"Reform," a new theme that was previously discussed and yet lacked a pivotal landmark, may finally be added. The Bauhaus, numerous Luther sites, and a steadily growing Great Pyramid would finally prove the region's outstanding potential, since hardly any other area could boast having launched three revolutions on a global scale.

Final Site Selection Criteria
Although Dessau-Roßlau is not an unsuitable habitat for the Great Pyramid, pursuing the project in a single location without considering alternatives would not be reasonable.

The final determination of the Great Pyramid´s location will take various criteria into consideration

Overall Criteria	Tourism Indicators	Home Market Indicators
broad global acceptance	number of international visitors	national market population
political stability	climate	cremation rate
legal environment	traffic connections	regional market population
availability and price of land	vicinity to major tourist attractions	
availability of investment grants		

The final location will have to be acceptable to customers in all substantial markets. It will be defined in a selection process after several municipalities and land owners from various countries have been invited to apply to host the Great Pyramid.

Exemplary Evaluation of Alternative Sites

Benchmarked against exemplary alternatives, Dessau-Roßlau exhibits a few obvious drawbacks. Above all, a very seasonal climate would make year-round operations of the Great Pyramid Park difficult, and the miniscule number of international tourists in the region would necessitate significantly larger marketing efforts than in many alternative locations.

Since the local law does not permit private operations of cemeteries, a public-private partnership with the City of Dessau-Roßlau would have to be implemented. A considerable advantage for the region is the availability of EU Economic Convergence funds of up to 30 percent of total investments. These funds, however, are also available in other European regions.

Benchmarked against alternatives, Saxony-Anhalt may not be the ideal location to host the Great Pyramid

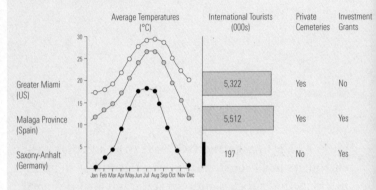

	Average Temperatures (°C)	International Tourists (000s)	Private Cemeteries	Investment Grants
Greater Miami (US)		5,322	Yes	No
Malaga Province (Spain)		5,512	Yes	Yes
Saxony-Anhalt (Germany)		197	No	Yes

Source: www.worldclimate.com, Government of Andalusia, Saxony-Anhalt Statistics Agency, Greater Miami Convention and Visitors Bureau, TGP analysis

INGO NIERMANN

Who is Borat?

At the beginning of 2007, we, the Friends of the Great Pyramid, began our search for a suitable location. In the economically underdeveloped eastern Germany, which we believed would especially profit from the expected employment effect through construction, operation, and guests, the search was soon narrowed to the towns of Dessau and Roßlau. For years, unemployment rates in the region have hovered at around 20 percent, and in July the two towns were supposed to unite in a measure that would, despite the rapid population shrinkage allow them to obtain big-city status with a collective 90,000 residents.

Dessau-Roßlau is located not far from the Elbe River, through which the necessary concrete ingredients might be shipped, and is only a good hour's drive by car from both the Berlin-Schönefeld and Leipzig/Halle airports. The Neue Dessauer Begräbnisplatz or New Dessau Burial Ground, built in 1787, was Germany's first graveyard without headstones and the Wörlitzer Garten is also in the immediate vicinity. Just like this venue—built in 1769 by Prince Leopold III Friedrich Franz von Anhalt-Dessau—was the first German park to be accessible to the public, the Great Pyramid is also not only accessible to one person, but to everyone as a potential gravesite. Though a pyramid construction within eyeshot of the Wörlitzer Garten could threaten the park's status as a UNESCO World Heritage Site, a proper distance of twenty or thirty kilometers would produce considerable synergy effects between the two landmarks.

In Streetz, a village of 250 residents, we found the largest unforested, undeveloped area in Dessau and Roßlau—too far from the Elbe to warrant fear of flooding. In February 2007, I paid a visit, together with documentary filmmaker Frauke Finsterwalder, who has been accompanying our project, to the deputy and later incumbent mayor Klaus Grünheidt and his wife Renate, head of the local rural women's association. Both appeared thrilled with the idea of erecting a pyramid in their village that could, even in much of the population's lifetime, grow to be a hundred meters and higher. Because, as they told us: "We love cultural monuments." They also looked forward to the documentary film and proudly pointed out that the local bakehouse association had already hosted visitors from a national television station. The mayor at the time, Dörte Liensdorf, could hardly wait for the pyramid to block the view of a windmill belonging to the neighboring village Mühlstedt. Reportedly one hundred meters tall, this old model had been freighted over after having been considered too loud for Bavaria. Perhaps it could be painted to go with the pyramid, like a palm tree.

It was only in May 2007, when we introduced the building plans to the village residents at the "Hummelstube," run by Dörte Liensdorf and her husband Willy-Michael, that a voice of dissent was raised. The first objection, offered by one older gentleman, was that even Chinese would come into the village. Non-native residents explained that they had come to live here for the nature, and now the view from their terrace would be a giant cement wall. The spokesman for the resistance dreaded the traffic that would clog the village street. We from the Friends of the Great Pyramid contended that a new road would of course have to be built from the nearest federal highway directly to the pyramid. And those who would choose not to live in the pyramid's close vicinity, unlike the case with the windmill, could expect not a loss but a considerable appreciation in value for their property and houses. The spokesman for the resistance thereupon laughingly declared that he, if offered half a million euros, would immediately sell his house. Evidently he thought this was highly unlikely.

It later came to light that the spokesman and many of the other pyramid antagonists didn't live in Streetz at all, but rather in Natho, a 110-resident neighboring village separated from Streetz by a wide forest belt. In the 1950s, Natho was annexed by the then still independent community of Streetz, and there were major tensions. Even at the beginning of the year, when the two village fire brigades were consolidated, the resentment was so great as to necessitate an intermediary intervention by the then mayor of Roßlau and current mayor of Dessau-Roßlau, Klemens Koschig.

While Mr. and Mrs. Liensdorf continued to advocate the pyramid, Klaus Grünheidt transformed himself into its open opponent. Rumors circulated throughout the village that one or the other had already sold land to us, the Friends of the Great Pyramid, and in fact Grünheidt does own a number of square acres in the area onto which the Great Pyramid could be built. Grünheidt had already made enemies when he approved the laying of a power supply line for the windmill through those very acres. Meanwhile the local evangelical pastor ranted that we, à la Borat, were only trying to make a spectacle of the villagers.

But who was using whom here? After all, a documentary film was made in which Streetz plays a major role. And Klaus Grünheidt was visibly pleased with the regular questions from press and television and could constantly come up with new theories against the pyramid. First he feared that the grave type would become so popular that the whole world would be covered in pyramids. I contested that in our scenario a single 500-meter-high pyramid offered space for around 190 million graves, and a one 1000-meter-high pyramid offered even enough space for over one and a half billion—in addition to that, the size of the individual stones could be reduced even more. Thereupon the new argument was: pressure from the pyramid would raise the ground level in Streetz by several meters. Grünheidt finally confided to the Frankfurter Allgemeine newspaper that a Berlin sect was behind the pyramid.

In the fall we organized a Pyramid Festival in Streetz at which we symbolically laid five prototype stones on the lot. Klaus Grünheidt, in good spirits, was one of the last to leave. Head mayor Klemens Koschig stayed even longer. When a little anti-demonstration paid their respects in the early evening and rammed a banner into the ground that read: "We don't want any 5,000,000 dead people in Streetz," and thus implied that the ashes of the dead are something akin to hazardous waste, Koschig eagerly defended the idea of the pyramid—simultaneously giving the all-clear: a construction proposal of this magnitude and length is not a decision for the city, but for the state of Saxony-Anhalt. There was therefore no need for action against the Great Pyramid. But something like the Pyramid Festival—something of that size won't be seen in Streetz for the next hundred years. In fact the young people that we met the day before at the Natho Fire Brigade Festival couldn't believe, no matter how many times we swore it was true, that the band Northern Lite was going to play for them here. Unpaid.

At the festival a young man approached me and assured me how great he thought the Great Pyramid was. If the people of Streetz didn't want it, why not just build it the next village over, in Mühlstedt?

LOCAL PROTESTERS AT THE GREAT PYRAMID FESTIVAL IN STREETZ.
PHOTO: INGO NIERMANN.

KATRIN HOLZBERGER FILMING THE BEGINNING OF HER STYROFOAM PYRAMID.
PHOTO: INGO NIERMANN.

DESIGN YOUR OWN PYRAMID STONE! PHOTO: STEFAN DIEFFENBACHER.

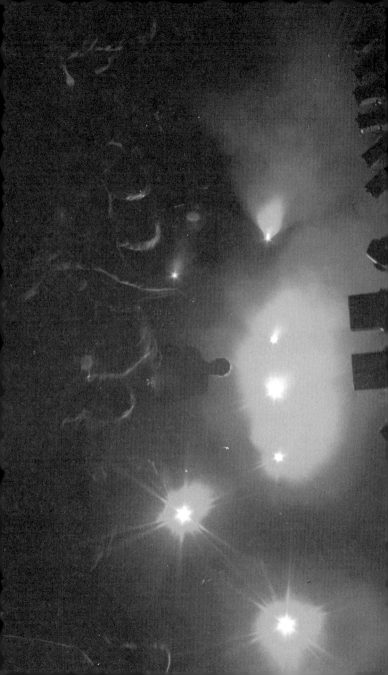

NORTHERN LITE PERFORMING. PHOTO: STEFAN DIEFFENBACHER.

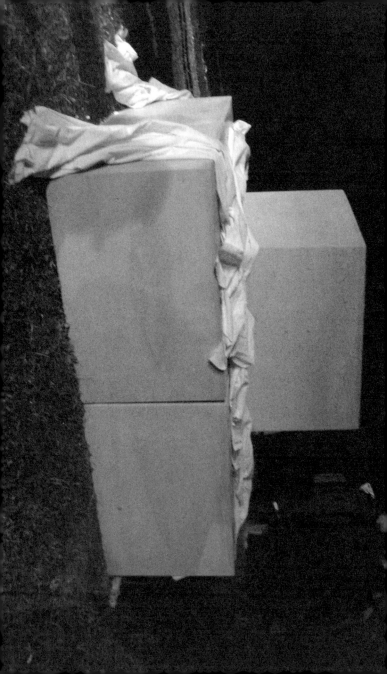

THE SYMBOLIC CORNERSTONES. PHOTO: VINCENT SCHMIDT.

INGO NIERMANN, JENS THIEL

A Call for Ideas

The Great Pyramid is the world's first monumental tomb and memorial site open to people of all nations, cultures, and religions. This competition calls for spatial and urban planning as well as other concepts able to convey the idea of "a monument for all of us"— a solution that reflects the pyramid's unifying force in a grand and growth-dynamic ensemble of surrounding buildings and landscapes.

Participants are invited to come forward with specific proposals extending beyond the given framework. Though additional proposals regarding the structure and building technology of the Great Pyramid are also welcome, entries should focus on aspects related to urban and spatial planning.

The competition objective is to specify high quality and unique, functional, and aesthetic strategies that are economically feasible to implement. The planning concepts should demonstrate the idea and the positive implications of the project to partners, decision makers, clients, and other stakeholders. The proponent's goal is to strongly foster and maximize the chances of the Great Pyramid's realization.

The special character of the project and situation require specific issues be taken into consideration:

Reverence and Remembrance

Outline, growth path, and building processes in the area as well as technologies must take into account the Great Pyramid's character as a memorial site. The impression the building makes should be appropriate and respectful. Designs should exhibit relations to—or at least be compatible with—funeral and memorial traditions of all large civilizations and religions.

Compatibility with Existing Structures

Proposals should consider existing settlements and cultural sites in the region and should also blend into the countryside. Although the monumentality of the Great Pyramid as a core structure in the area cannot and should not be camouflaged, it should relate smoothly to existing structures. Preferably, the inhabitants of rural settlements within a five-kilometer radius should experience positive impacts from the project instead of losing quality of life when building and tourism take off. Adequate (new) traffic connections will be a crucial part of ensuring this condition. The cultural heritage sites in a thirty-kilometer radius around the area are pivotal points in the region's tourism marketing concepts. Establishing relationships with these sites, thereby echoing self-perception of the region, can significantly increase the project's chances of realization.

Consideration of Growth Dynamics

Proposals should take into account the strong dynamics of building and tourism. Beginning with only a few thousand stones and visitors per year, the Great Pyramid area must be able to deal with figures exponentially higher than those after only a few years. The growth dynamics of the project are uncertain and based on educated estimates. Therefore, flexibility to react to changing capacities without reducing economic efficiency will be a crucial assessment criterion.

Attraction of Tourists and Mourners

The area should enhance the perception of the Great Pyramid as a major tourist attraction without belittling its character as a memorial site. The design and sojourn quality of the area should not only be able to cope with high numbers of visitors, but also actively attract guests. Visitors should become increasingly excited and enthusiastic as they approach the Great Pyramid, and should sense the grandeur of the area even if they arrive grief-stricken after the loss of a close relative or friend. They should find reason to spend more than just an hour or two once they have arrived. A visitors center adapting to an increasing number of guests seems pivotal in this concept.

Rites and Memorial Practices

In order for the Great Pyramid to serve as a memorial site accessible to the wider public, new rites and memorial practices will have to be designed and established. Since the setting of a stone in the building structure might not be directly witnessed by the public because of safety issues, new ceremonies engaging in other stages of the process will be needed. Due to the fact that stones will only be openly visible on the Great Pyramid's surface for a few months, new forms of memorial will also have to be established. These forms could range from a memorial wall listing names to multimedia installations dedicated to people honored in the Great Pyramid. Entrants are encouraged to provide their own ideas and to sketch the respective processes.

Adaptility

Notwithstanding the fact that Dessau-Roßlau is for various reasons an ideal location for the project, it is uncertain whether the local authorities will, ultimately, issue a building permit. Participants in the competition are therefore encouraged to use site-independent or modular approaches to planning that might also be applied to other locations.

THE COMPETITION SITE. PHOTO: INGO NIERMANN.

ATELIER BOW-WOW

Void Metabolism

Yoshiharu Tsukamoto, Momoyo Kaijima, and Simon Morville with Kei Matsuda, Nicolas Croze, Florian de Visser, and Simon Persson

The extraordinary context of the Great Pyramid encouraged us to create a new type of city based on the concept of void metabolism. Unlike the core characteristics of the metabolist movement in the 1960s, void metabolism constantly evolves. Instead of static form and function, it allows changes of elements and structure at the same time, responding to the surrounding context. Elements are detached and linkages locally defined, facilitating flexible growth through arrangements of repetitive units. In this way, development follows the same exponential growth as the pyramid, progressively forming a linear city in a ring around the pyramid that follows the limits of the site.

The pyramid is the epicenter of the site, around which all elements gravitate. They give context to the pyramid, embedding it in the landscape through ritual. Death is part of the cycle of life that pushes humanity and all living species to evolve constantly, and the void metabolist city is conceived in this spirit: to allow any possible evolution in the future. It suggests a strategy of implantation, which can support any possible functions and easily adapt to the growth of the project, while offering the chance for people to interact and commune with each other.

Following this main idea, we propose an unlimited number of scenarios from eight elements that compose our project.

Infra Ring

The ring is the infrastructure dedicated to the new flux generated by the pyramid. It circumnavigates the boundary of the site, connecting to the two main existing roads and distributing the linear city all along its inner periphery. The impact of the fluxes is minimized to preserve the living conditions of the local dwellers by bypassing the existing villages and following existing roads and paths as far as possible. Parking is integrated into the ring every kilometer, and there are four roads for stone delivery, each connecting to one of the four canals. Programmatic functions such as these are integrated into the ring with a consistently changing road width.

Leaf-Bedrooms and Leaf-Facilities

Inspired by the diversity of shapes from Herman de Vries' work of art, we created a diagram of leaf-architectural typologies adapted to our programmatic intentions. There are two main types of rooms: bedrooms and facilities, each of which have the potential to be any shape.

The bedrooms are treated as ritual spaces, where a visitor spending a night on the site can meditate while facing the pyramid landscape. Each room has its own individual path that eventually connects to the pyramid, forming a special connection between the guest and the monument. The facilities connect to the promenade and serve as spaces for both everyday requirements and spiritual endeavors. The necropolis is dedicated to the memory of the deceased, but also allows the continuation of life in a poetic and unique atmosphere.

Linear City

The linear city roughly follows the inside of the ring with a setback of two hundred meters, as a first transition into the pyramid territory. Void space is the main spatial quality of the new urban space; the varying densities of detached elements spontaneously form a promenade with clusters of leaf-bedrooms oriented toward the pyramid on the inside, and with leaf-facilities oriented toward the ring on the outside. The leaf typologies are presented as a metaphor of the volumes that compose void metabolism: in fact, they could be any shape, as the essence lies in the layout of detached elements generating a pattern of void spaces interacting freely. Void metabolism generates a maximum fluidity of movement and also creates multiple angles of views through interstitial spaces. This permeability of space impulsively leads the visitors toward the tree-paths and the pyramid.

Stone River

After being deposited on the ring by truck, the stones move slowly toward the construction site by canal, as a last symbolic journey through the purifying element of water. The boat becomes the private ceremonial space where the friends and relatives of the departed can reflect, meditate, and be in contact with the stone.

Four canals span across the fields from the ring to the pyramid construction platform. Existing and artificial changes in topography around the site create dramatic views both from and of the canals, allowing other visitors to observe the flow of stone in the landscape.

Tree-Paths to the Linear City

The tree-paths take root at each corner of the pyramid's construction platform and ramify until they reach the linear city. The width of the paths changes at each ramification, from the narrow path attached to the leaf-bedroom to the broad trunk rooted in the construction platform. We imagined a twice-daily procession fixed at sunrise and sunset, in which visitors leave the linear city on small individual paths and progressively gather as the paths get wider, finally reaching the pyramid together.

Void Space of Gardens and Fields

The geometry of the tree paths generates a variety of fields, from small cultivated gardens, to agricultural scale crop and flower fields, to vast plains of pastureland and untamed flora.

Produce from the fields can be used in the linear city's restaurants, bakeries, and flower shops, creating a partially self-sufficient microcosmic ecosystem. Some fields throughout the site are regularly burned, while others are kept until they reach the state of climax vegetation; the fallow fields show different stages of the natural cycle as a continuous rebirth of life. Some fields and gardens may be used by an invited artist for a sculpture or as a site for landscape art. This textured landscape offers thousands of possible journeys through different environments, all gathering for the final approach to the pyramid.

Memorial Wall Gallery

The gallery frames the pyramid, connected to the tree-paths at its corners and to the canals at its sides. It faces out onto the construction platform, allowing visitors to watch the ongoing construction work. The earth-sheltered back wall is carved with names of the deceased, creating a memorial wall that lines the gallery. The gallery also acts as a harbor for visitors accompanying the stones by boat; during the construction period, only visitors attending a stone ceremony will be able to enter the construction platform, but without the option of stepping out onto it. As the canals lay on different topographic levels, the gallery is composed of four wings: two opposite wings lie on the ground at the highest and lowest levels, and the two other wings are sloped to connect them. This situation of different levels allows a variety of viewpoints to observe the construction and to witness the stone of a beloved one being laid on the edifice.

Construction Platform & Memorial Plaza

The construction platform is the surface directly surrounding the pyramid, only accessible to the workers until the completion of the monument, when the platform becomes a public plaza. During the construction, visitors can observe the placing of stones from the adjoining gallery.

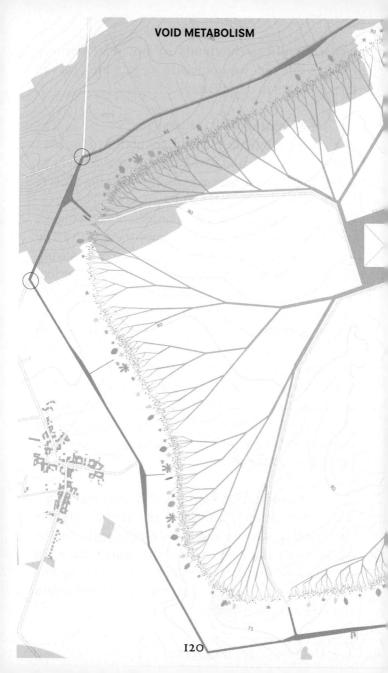

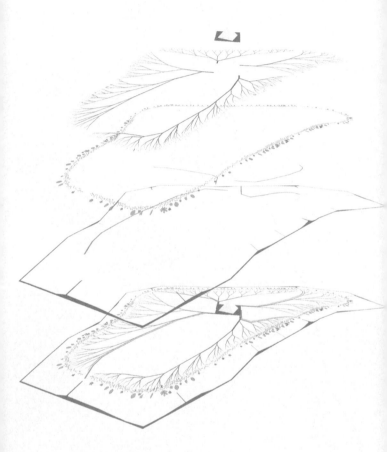

VOID METABOLISM

Geriatric Space

*Project Team: Nikolaus Hirsch, Wolfgang Lorch,
Markus Miessen, Valeska Bühler, Matthias Görlich,
Santiago Espitia Berndt; Structural Engineering:
Bollinger & Grohmann*

Geriatric Space:

A Brief for a Zone Between Life and Death

Contemporary societies still focus on the cult of youth, yet slowly but inevitably the discourse is acknowledging the demographic facts of the aging population. The new question is: How does a society react to a reality in which age and death shift into its center? How does a society organize spaces that negotiate the dead and the living? Is it still possible to define those spaces as "heterotopian," i.e. as Foucault did when he described the modern invention of hospitals, asylums, and cemeteries? Can we develop spaces that include age and death and understand them not through notions of decay but as a trigger for urban development?

Based on the pyramid as its urban catalyst, the project in question creates a zone between life and death, a city of passing away, without being marginalized by the societies from which its inhabitants originate. The urban addresses the question of how one can think of environments that produce a quality of homeliness. The vast majority of people tend to think of death as something that can be postponed, something that is not to be addressed within one's lifetime. However, with more and more people suffering from terminal illnesses, one needs to think about scenarios in which people can not only immerse themselves in environments of care, but further, about how they relate with the space where they will eventually be buried. The question arises as to what could potentially turn those spaces into typologies that are no longer connected with fear and despair, but with both solitude and community.

Until now, we seem to have failed to have produced the necessary links between what one might call the "environment of home" and the "environment of death." In order to generate a rupture within the homogeneity of the kinds of care environments to which we are accustomed, a new space is needed—one that is comprised of a mix of international residents, visitors, and service personnel: a multi-language, multi-ethnic, and a-territorial population.

pyramid

funeral parlour

flower shop

bereavement

crematory

precast concrete manufactory

interim storage for stones

administration

parking

tv studio

documentation / life long learning centre

hotel

nursing home

home for the terminally ill

cryonics institute

500 n

Necro-Urbanism

The ancient monuments of death such as the Egyptian pyramids and the Valley of the Kings have been more than just isolated objects in the sand. They were part of an entire necropolis, a large-scale urban space that included all sorts of different activities. In the contemporary space of the twentieth and twenty-first centuries, new "themed" spaces and urban developments appeared: the VW Autostadt, Dubai's 2.5-million-square-meter Healthcare City (the world's first healthcare free zone), and the gambling city Las Vegas. Could the pyramid project originate a "Las Vegas of Death"?

Healthcare City, Dubai

Giza pyramid complex

Reciprocal Growth Process: Pyramid & Site

The material strategy of the pyramid establishes a conceptual link with the site. The growing pyramid gradually transforms the site. 30 percent of the cement mass that is necessary for the construction of the pyramid is gained from ground that eventually mutates into a lake. The more the pyramid grows, the more the lake expands. Positive and negative volumes are reciprocal.

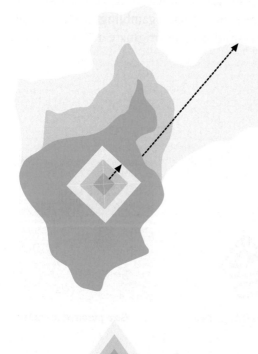

HIRSCH/LORCH/MIESSEN

The Structural System of the Pyramid

The traditional, massive structural system of the pyramid evolves into a complex, more porous geometry that reduces its material density. Based on a masonry system that avoids flush geometries, concrete stones alternate with gaps and holes. The structural stiffness between the different layers of the growth process is achieved through the interconnection of stones turned ninety degrees. These operations reduce the structural weight and—as a side effect—will allow the pyramid to reach its full volume faster than would a completely solid pyramid. Contrary to the homogeneity of the old pyramid as a one-person monument, the complexity of the new modular system enhances the individuality of tomb and memory stones.

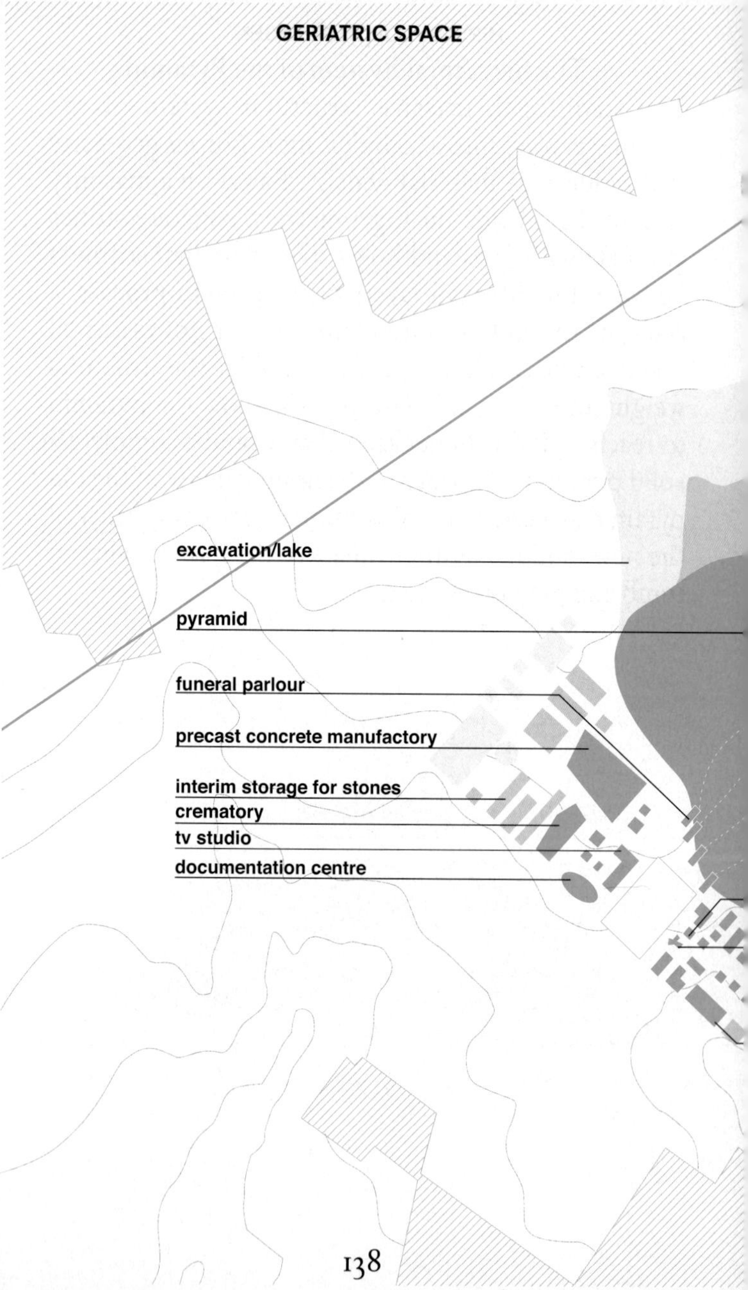

excavation/lake

pyramid

funeral parlour

precast concrete manufactory

interim storage for stones
crematory
tv studio
documentation centre

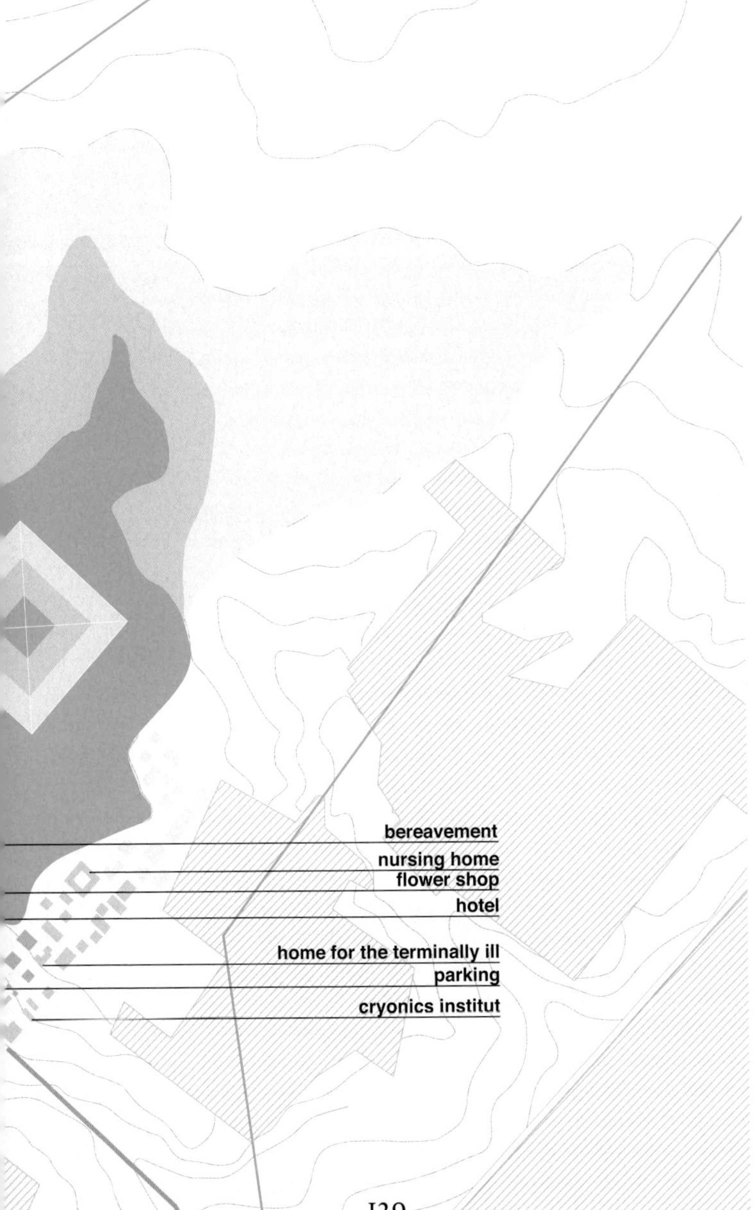

bereavement
nursing home
flower shop
hotel

home for the terminally ill
parking
cryonics institut

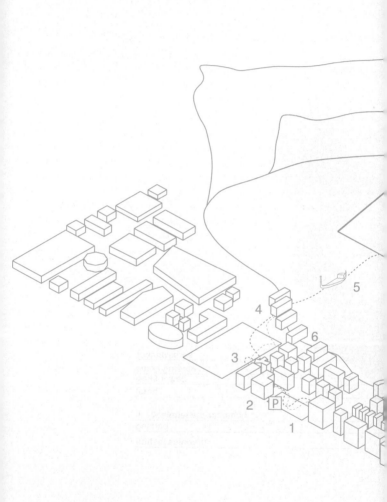

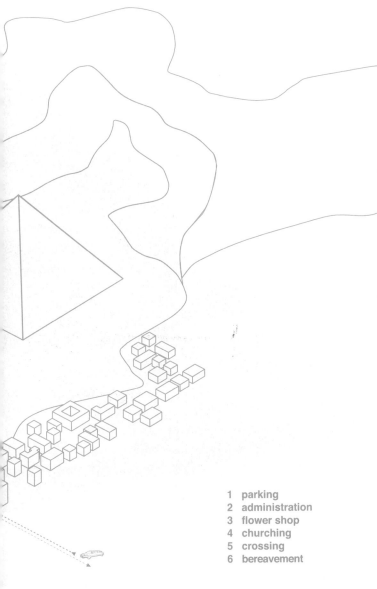

1 parking
2 administration
3 flower shop
4 churching
5 crossing
6 bereavement

Life and Death Interact

Ai Weiwei, Phil Dunn, Henri van Hoeve,
Babul Vazhoor, Cia Shi Chen

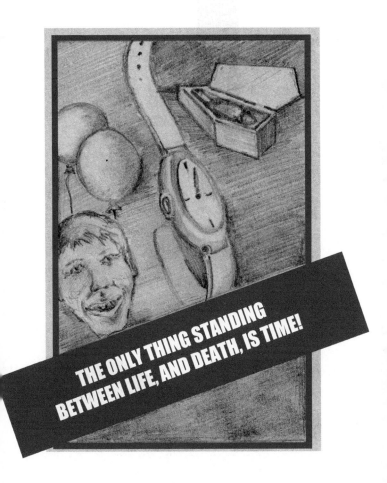

THE ONLY THING STANDING BETWEEN LIFE, AND DEATH, IS TIME!

LIFE AND DEATH INTERACT

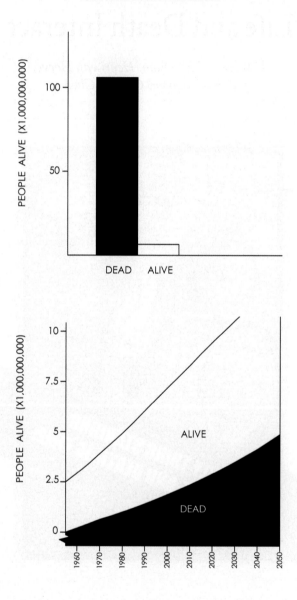

BE PATIENT...

EMBRACE THE INEVITABILITY...

YOU HAVE TO LIVE BEFORE YOU CAN DIE

BALANCE

INTEGRATION

LEARNING TO GIVE IS LEARNING TO RECEIVE...

YOU ARE PART OF SOMETHING BIGGER...

CONTRIBUTE YOUR LIFE...

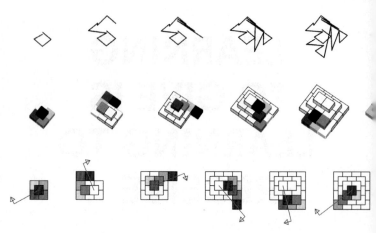

SPIRALING GROWTH OF THE GREAT PYRAMID

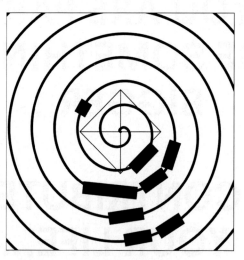

SPIRALING GROWTH OF THE GREAT PYRAMID PARK

FAKE DESIGN

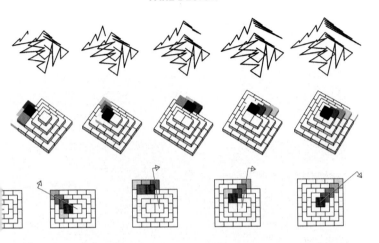

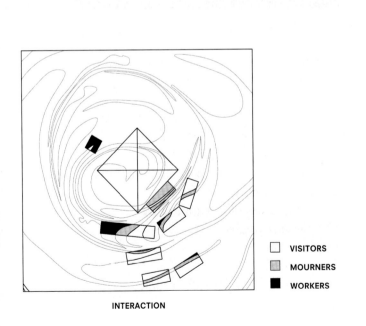

VISITORS
MOURNERS
WORKERS

INTERACTION

Workers
The light of dawn has just broken ground
A shadow extends across the horizon
The mammoth grows
At the hands of those who now approach
Arrival marks the onslaught of contribution,
The strain and sweat given in life
To stack this celebration to those no more
The responsibility of each part
The recognition of its significance
The pleasure to give
To give a day
A day retired
And hopes of another still to come

Visitors
The excitement builds
Driven like a wedge
Piercing the blue above
The destination appears
Transforming from a solid
The pixels of past life reveal themselves
Joined is the celebration of what was
And what is
The division blurred
Feeling life's every sensation
Straining to an extreme
Knowing that you are
Embracing that it is not eternal
Surrounded by those who live
Confronted by those who do not
Loving the possession of life

Mourners
The pavement sprawls ahead
Rising out of the horizon
A force of magnetism
Drawn within its shade
A space of celebration
Where opposites converge
And the proximity of one
Shines light on its counterpart
The line between the two fades
We smile for the beauty of the sequence
And with fulfillment back away
Prepared but not ready.

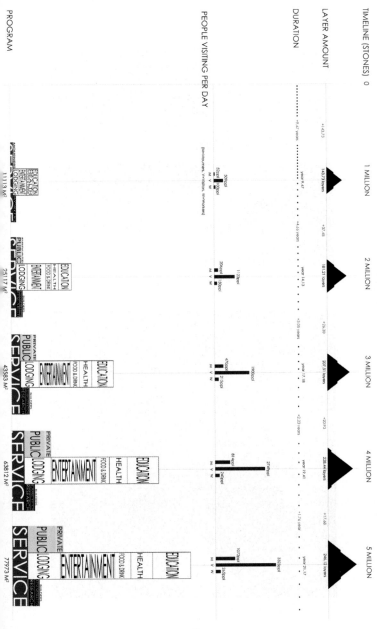

LIFE AND DEATH INTERACT

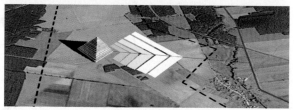

PHASES OF GROWTH

SITE PLAN

JOIN THE MOVEMENT, BE REMEMBERED...

CHOOSE DEATH!

ARE YOU DYING TO BE PART OF SOMETHING BIGGER?

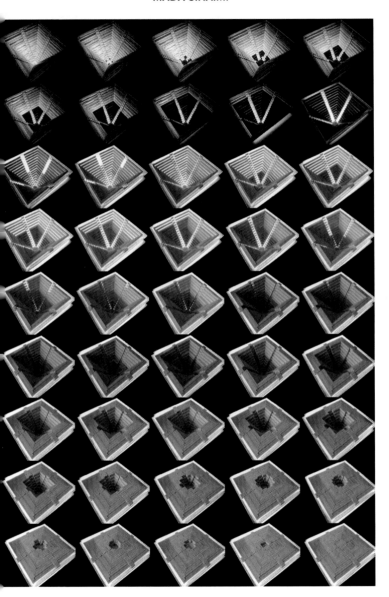

DIMARYP

172

MADA S.P.A.M.

ONE WAY →

REM KOOLHAAS

Jury Decision: Four Winners

AT FIRST, THE FRIENDS OF THE GREAT
PYRAMID CONCEIVED OF THE ARCHITECTURE
CONTEST AS AN OPEN, PRIMARILY STUDENT-
ORIENTED CALL FOR PROPOSALS, A CONTEST
WITH A 3000-EURO CASH PRIZE. THEN, WHEN
REM KOOLHAAS AGREED TO JOIN THE JURY,
HE ADVOCATED A CLOSED COMPETITION AS
A WAY OF MOTIVATING PARTICIPATION FROM
IN-DEMAND ARCHITECTURE FIRMS. THE PRIZE
MONEY WAS CANCELLED IN LIEU OF 1000
EUROS OF STARTING MONEY, GIVEN TO COVER
AT LEAST THE MATERIAL AND SHIPPING COSTS
FOR THE FIVE INVITED FIRMS: AI WEIWEI/FAKE
DESIGN, ARQUITECTONICA GEO, ATELIER BOW-
WOW, NIKOLAUS HIRSCH, WOLFGANG LORCH
& MARKUS MIESSEN, AND MADA S.P.A.M. EACH
FIRM SUBMITTED THEIR DESIGNS ON TIME;
ARQUITECTONICA GEO WAS THE ONLY ONE TO
WITHDRAW FROM THE COMPETITION A FEW
DAYS BEFORE THE DEADLINE. ON JANUARY
22, 2008 AT 3 P.M., MEMBERS OF A JURY THAT
INCLUDED OMAR AKBAR (ARCHITECT AND
EXECUTIVE DIRECTOR OF THE BAUHAUS
DESSAU FOUNDATION), STEFANO BOERI
(ARCHITECT AND EDITOR-IN-CHIEF OF
ABITARE), REM KOOLHAAS (ARCHITECT AND
FOUNDING PARTNER OF OMA, THE OFFICE
FOR METROPOLITAN ARCHITECTURE), INGO
NIERMANN (WRITER, FRIENDS OF THE GREAT
PYRAMID), AND MIUCCIA PRADA (DESIGNER
AND ENTREPRENEUR) MET IN THE LATTER'S
MILAN OFFICE, A LARGE ROOM WITH GRAY
CONCRETE FLOORING AND BARE WHITE
WALLS. THE JURY TOOK THEIR SEATS AT A
SMALL CONFERENCE TABLE WITH ORANGE-
COLORED PLASTIC SHELL CHAIRS AND

STUDIED THE DESIGNS, PRINTED ON A0 PAPER.
THOUGH THE BLINDS WERE DRAWN, THE
LATE WINTER SUNLIGHT PIERCED BRIGHTLY
THROUGH THE SLATS. A VALET WHEELED A
SERVING TABLE INTO THE ROOM WITH TEA,
COFFEE, FRESH ORANGE JUICE, AND FRUIT.
AFTER AN INTENSIVE DISCUSSION THAT
LASTED SEVERAL HOURS, THE JURY REACHED
A DECISION AND STRETCHED THEIR LEGS
ON A LAWN AND DAISY-PLANTED TERRACE.
ONLY REM KOOLHAAS REMAINED SEATED TO
SUMMARIZE THE DECISION, AS FOLLOWS,
IN WRITING.

The Jury of the Great Pyramid competition spent a long afternoon studying proposals. They were impressed, not only by the caliber of the individual entries, but even more by the way the architects' works were further reinforcements of the value of *Umbauland's* initial hypothesis.

Niermann's story addressed the poverty and confusion of our current attitudes toward death but also tantalizingly suggested that a specific zone on a specific German location in a specific moment in history could be dedicated to a monumental effort to find a new way doing justice to both the dead and the living. In other words, he accepted political implications of his work and asked architects to keep developing it.

The projects each contribute important elements to reinforce Niermann's initial hypothesis. They differ not so much in architectural language, but in methodology and exploration of very complementary aspects.

Fake contributed significant thinking on the construction of the pyramid and the way memory could "work." They also suggested a language both plausible and profound, in which the entire complex could be advertised or even branded independent of any design.

Bow-Wow's project establishes a new poetic way to relate life and death. The pyramid becomes the center of a meditation "village," where both individual memory and the massive presence of death are balanced across a delicate landscape of ritual.

Nikolaus Hirsch, Wolfgang Lorch & Markus Miessen demonstrate the feasibility of the pyramid's original thesis by extracting from our current daily life the elements dedicated not only to death, but also to the vast industries that surround it. They reassemble these elements in a programmatic organization surrounding a lake with a pyramid-lite in its center, which removes some of the dead weight associated with the form.

MADA's project explores a space far beyond Niermann's initial model by suggesting for the first time in three thousand years an exploration of the pyramid's inside, in a hallucinatory journey across the Elbe that ends eventually in a reintegration with the landscape.

The three first projects each contain elements susceptible to play a role in the eventual implementation of the pyramid and to produce ammunition for a campaign. In the end, the variety and richness of the entries kept the jury from declaring a single winner. Given the enormity of the enterprise, there is scope for each author to contribute and enrich the massive effort.

GRAPHIC DESIGNER ZAK KYES PROPOSES A CAMPAIGN FOR THE GREAT PYRAMID.
DRAFT, 2008.

GRAPHIC DESIGNER ZAK KYES PROPOSES A CAMPAIGN FOR THE GREAT PYRAMID.
REVISED DRAFT, 2008. WWW.THECHOICES.NET

Ingo Niermann, *1969 in Bielefeld, Germany,
currently lives in Berlin. He is a novelist, freelance
writer, and editor of *Solution*. His published books
include *China ruft dich* (2008), *Metan* (with Christian
Kracht, 2007), *Breites Wissen—Die seltsame Welt der
Drogen und ihrer Nutzer* (with Adriano Sack, 2007),
Umbauland—Zehn deutsche Visionen (2006), *Skarbek*
(with Antje Majewski, 2005), *Atomkrieg* (with Antje
Majewski, 2004), *Minusvisionen—Unternehmer ohne
Geld* (2003), and *Der Effekt* (2001).

Jens Thiel, *1970 in Bergen auf Rügen, Germany,
is an entrepreneur-cum-artist currently living in Berlin
and Erfurt. He studied economics and business in
Germany, the UK, and Russia; founded one of
the first German coffee bar systems in the mid-1990s;
and has worked as a consultant for various Internet
companies and strategic management consulting
firms. In addition to the Great Pyramid, he is currently
working on an extensive research and publication
project about the monobloc plastic chair, the most
successful and most unloved piece of furniture of
all human creation.

Heiko Holzberger, *1965 in Steinach/Thüringen,
Germany, is a civil engineer and research associate at
the Bauhaus University in Weimar. For over fifteen
years, he has investigated the academic, economic, and
sociopolitical aspects of infrastructure planning.
In addition to research and lecturing, Holzberger also
works as a consulting engineer with a special emphasis
on transport planning.

Chus Martínez, *1972, critic and curator, is currently director of the Frankfurter Kunstverein in Frankfurt, Germany.

Christian Kracht, *1966, is a Swiss cultural theorist.

Till Huber, *1978, is a literary scholar and lives in Hamburg, Germany. His research focuses are aestheticism and German-language pop music.

Hans Ulrich Obrist, *1968, is one of the most eccentric producers of meaning in the art world. A nonstop interviewer, his curatorial jumpstart began with a show in his kitchen.

David Woodard, *1964, Conductor and Music Director of the Los Angeles Chamber Group, divides his time between Germany and South America.

Atelier Bow-Wow was established by Yoshiharu Tsukamoto, *1965, and Momoyo Kaijima, *1969, in Tokyo in 1992.

Nikolaus Hirsch, *1964, is an architect based in Frankfurt.

Wolfgang Lorch, *1960, is an architect and co-founder of Wandel Hoefer Lorch, Germany.

Markus Miessen, *1978, is a London-based architect, researcher, educator, and writer.

FAKE Design was established by artist Ai Weiwei, *1957, in Beijing in 1999.

MADA s.p.a.m. was established by Ma Qingyun, *1965, in Shanghai in 2000.

Rem Koolhaas, *1944, is founding partner of the Office for Metropolitan Architecture (OMA).

Zak Kyes, *1983, is a Swiss-American graphic designer living in London. He is Art Director of the Architectural Association and has curated the exhibition *Forms of Inquiry: The Architecture of Critical Graphic Design* and co-edited the accompanying publication (with Mark Owens, 2007).

COLOPHON

Solution 9: The Great Pyramid is part of the *Solution* series edited by Ingo Niermann and designed by Zak Kyes.

ISBN 978-1-933128-43-6

Editors: Ingo Niermann, Jens Thiel
Translators: Amy Patton, April Lamm
Copy editors: Penny Eifrig, Courtney Johnson
German copy editor: Sabine Grimm

Designer: Zak Kyes
zakgroup.co.uk

Printed and bound by Die Keure in Belgium.

Sternberg Press
Caroline Schneider
Karl-Marx-Allee 78, D-10243 Berlin
1182 Broadway #1602, New York NY 10001
www.sternberg-press.com

Funded by:

gefördert im programm
ARBEIT IN ZUKUNFT

ACKNOWLEDGEMENTS

The German Federal Cultural Foundation, most especially Uta Schnell and Friederike Tappe-Hornbostel, and members of the jury at the German Federal Culture Foundation's "Future of Labour" program who voted for our project.

Our fellow campaigners Heiko Holzberger, Stefan Dieffenbacher, René Eisfeld, Daniel Windheuser, Rainer Köllgen, Peter Seeberg, and Alexander Wolf.

The founding members of the Friends of the Great Pyramid: Maik Bluhm, Katrin Holzberger, Christian Kracht (ex), and Antje Majewski.

Franziska Föhse, Peter Kunath, Tobias Rahm, Sindy Schicht, and Claudia Weißberg for their technical studies. Dr. Gerd Häselbarth and the F.A. Finger Institut at Bauhaus University Weimar. Thomas Rehder & Betoniu for the test stones.

The participants in the architectural competition and the following jury members: Omar Akbar, Stefano Boeri, Rem Koolhaas, and Miuccia Prada.

Zak Kyes for the book design and Elisabeth Schulze for the charts.

Caroline Schneider and Tatjana Günthner at Sternberg Press.

The designer would like to thank Markus Miessen, Wouter Rummens, and Tine Vanhee in addition to Phill Clatworthy and Lina Maria Grumm, who assisted in the design of this book.

Klaus Altenkirch, Kaspar Althaus & Aveato Business Catering, Christoph de Babalon, the Bahlmann family, Christoph Bartel, Sebastian Bohn & Northern Lite, Frieda Bilitza †, Vera Brannen, Dörte Brese, Jochen Büchner, Stefanie Carp, Simon Deichsel, Bill Drummond, Frauke Finsterwalder, Jens Friebe, Klaus Grünheidt, Ulrich Haage, Carl Hegemann, Sonja Hildebrandt, Juli Holz, Till Huber, Michael Kieslow, Jan Knikker, Alexander Korte, Martin Koschlig †, Gero Kutzner, April Lamm, Götz Leineweber, Dörte and Willy-Michael Liensdorf, David Lieske, Matthias Lilienthal, Paola Maggi, Patrick Martin, Chus Martínez, Paola Nicolin, Erik Niedling, Christoph Normann & wrapstars Event Management, Jonas Obleser, Hans Ulrich Obrist, Amy Patton, Gianluigi Ricuperati, Steffen Ritter, Stefanie Roenneke, Phillip Sollmann, Roßlauer Streetkids, Wolfgang Schmieder, Vincent Schmidt, Dirk Spielberg, Spielmannszug Blau-Weiß Roßlau, Sieglinde Thiel, Stephan Trüby, Katrin Vellrath, Madelon Vriesendorp, Ronnie Vuine, Tobias Walker, Christian von Werner, David Woodard and the Los Angeles Chamber Group, Martin Ziegler & Live Veranstaltungstechnik.